Solitary Genius

Discovering the Gifted Child Within

A Memoir

by
Mo Marshall

iUniverse, Inc.
New York Bloomington

Solitary Genius

Discovering the Gifted Child Within

A Memoir

Copyright © 2008 by Mo Marshall

All rights reserved. No part of this book may be used or reproduced by any means, graphic, electronic, or mechanical, including photocopying, recording, taping or by any information storage retrieval system without the written permission of the publisher except in the case of brief quotations embodied in critical articles and reviews.

iUniverse books may be ordered through booksellers or by contacting:

iUniverse
1663 Liberty Drive
Bloomington, IN 47403
www.iuniverse.com
1-800-Authors (1-800-288-4677)

Because of the dynamic nature of the Internet, any Web addresses or links contained in this book may have changed since publication and may no longer be valid. The views expressed in this work are solely those of the author and do not necessarily reflect the views of the publisher, and the publisher hereby disclaims any responsibility for them.

ISBN:978-0-595-53472-2 (pbk)
ISBN: 978-1-4401-1015-3 (cloth)
ISBN: 978-0-595-63530-6 (ebk)

Printed in the United States of America

iUniverse rev. date: 6/2/2009

Names have been changed for the privacy of those written about unless consent was given to use actual names. This is the honest account of my childhood and early years just out of college. I am not a doctor and I no longer work in speech pathology and, therefore, I am not suggesting that the methods discussed within these pages are a "cure" for anyone.

For my extraordinary cousin who not only helped me get on my feet in New York City, but was an example of how to live with class and heart:

Phyllis Huffman DelVecchio
Your Spirit lives on

and

To The first person who told me this book was meant to be:

Sonia Choquette

Preface

When I sat down to write this book, which intended to recount the year I spent teaching kids who have severe communication and social problems, I had no idea that I was in part writing about myself.

I was a recent college grad, fresh out of Loyola College with a speech pathology degree in hand. I got a job working for a remarkable woman, first with her privately, then as the teacher of a new special needs class in a private school that was under her auspices.

When school first started, I worked in a computer room with one child who could barely make eye contact or speak. By the end of the school term, we had our own classroom and we were a team of eight. (I had a teaching assistant at this point, an angel named Suri.)

Here's what was so astounding about that magical year. These kids, all of whom had lived on the margins of society, began to blossom and come out of their shells and move into the larger, public world that the rest of us inhabit. As each of them made this transition from cocoon to butterfly, I did, too. It took being around these remarkable, lovable kids to realize I was — or had been — one of them myself.

As I began to put their stories down on paper, I found myself revisiting my own childhood, which had been very lonely and very difficult — especially where school was concerned. I, too, just didn't fit in and I, too, just wanted to retreat into my own world, my own head, my own place of safety.

I was the fourth of ten children, born to parents who meant well but who had their own limitations. Given my need for lots of alone time and craving one-on-one attention, home was often lonelier than any place else on earth for me.

What I learned working with those children and what I learned about myself transformed me: given the right kind of nurturance, which consists of compassion, patience, and true listening—all in equal measure—we all begin to feel accepted and loved and can overcome astounding obstacles—even hurdles that many believe will keep us marginalized for life.

Though I was, ostensibly, the teacher during that incredible year, it was I who truly learned about the boundless capacity of the human heart and how, when we follow our instincts and act from a place of love, we can truly make a difference in the lives of another and in the world.

It is my hope that my story, and the story of these beautiful kids, will inspire and transform you, too.

– Mo Marshall

Contents

1. 1
2. 5
3. 9
4. 17
5. 27
6. 31
7. 37
8. 41
9. 47
10. 51
11. 53
12. 55
13. 61
14. 65
15. 69
16. 73
17. 79
18. 83
19. 91
20. 95
21. 97
22. 101
23. 105
24. 109
25. 115

1

I searched the racks of Banana Republic feeling completely at a loss as to what to wear. I had already been to Ann Taylor and had found nothing. Sighing, I looked up and saw that Talbots had just opened an outlet store in the mall. I associated Talbots with my mother, so I went in with great hesitation. I found my first suit that was not completely unfashionable but was the perfect shade of light green to complement my eyes and skin color. I found a pair of killer Donna Karan heels, which would last a lifetime and offset the discomfort I had with the thought of wearing a full suit.

The interview was a success. I got the job working as an assistant to a doctor of speech pathology. It was 1997 and I had just graduated with a BA in speech pathology, the discipline that focuses on therapy for young children and adults, so this was ideal. Judith was petite, only about five feet tall. She reminded me of my mother because she always walked quickly and spoke loudly with a smile.

I learned that the bulk of my job would be assisting children playing computer games in Judith's office, located on the basement level of her luxurious townhouse. However, these were no ordinary computer games. The program was developed at Rutgers University. It was a cutting-edge technology designed for learning disabled children with auditory processing difficulties. Each child began the 8 to 12 week program by taking a computerized assessment test. From this initial assessment, the speed at which a child processed information was noted. Each game began at the child's processing speed and slowly increased by milliseconds, with the goal of eventually being able to process sound at a normal rate. The idea behind the technology was that it would retrain parts of the brain to process spoken language more quickly and accurately.

Children came in anywhere from 8:30 in the morning until 6 at night to accommodate their hectic summer schedules and complete their one hour and forty minutes of intense and continuous game playing. When I first began working with Judith, she was not prescribing this program for children with autism, but only for those with more mild learning disabilities.

I could have as many as four children at once. The personality differences of each of these children complemented the range and degrees of their learning disabilities. Some children sat down with their snack, put on their headphones and worked in silence for the full hour and forty minutes. Some balked and complained and found every excuse to get up. Others were outwardly rude and defiant. I wasn't sure if I would know how to deal with each and every one of them. I kept in mind my own experience growing up as the fourth of ten children.

From the start, I always stayed longer than I was asked to and did so without resentment. Judith immediately saw my commitment and kindness toward each child. I also believe she recognized that I had good instincts with the children. I had learned from growing up with my younger siblings that you had to establish a connection or they would rebel. I understood that it had to be clear that the only acceptable behavior was kindness toward each other. As a result, Judith deduced that I had good intentions and was a capable, hard worker.

A signal of her confidence in me came when she asked me if I would be interested in teaching a pilot program for children with autism and other severe speech and language disorders. She was going to start her pilot program at a nearby private school. I accepted her offer with some uncertainty; I didn't know how to teach these children. She assured me she would be there to guide me.

The premise of my teaching would be based on principles derived from speech and language pathology. I was unsure of how I was going to do this for an entire school day as I had only been exposed to one-on-one therapy sessions that lasted no more than an hour long. Judith explained that she would show me when my first student came to visit for a private speech session. She assured me she would demonstrate how to speak with Andrew and I would be fine from there on.

One summer afternoon, Andrew scampered down the stairs and into the waiting area. He was an adorable 4-year-old who was diagnosed with Pervasive Developmental Disorder (PDD). He was petite, like his mother, and almost had the look of a munchkin from *The Wizard of Oz*. As soon as Judith was ready, he slipped into her office. It consisted of a couch, a table, and built-in shelves with toys she could easily reach. The most noticeable part of the session was how she stated out loud exactly what Andrew was doing. "Andrew is putting the dinosaur on the table."

Andrew was inspired by his dinosaur and continued to create things for his dinosaur to do. Judith was sure to verbalize all of these things.

I partially understood her method of therapy. I knew that children learn best when they choose a preferred task. In my eyes, this was what Judith was doing in her session. She allowed Andrew to choose, yet in her mind she clearly controlled the objective she wanted him to reach. It was a careful balancing act. I didn't know if I could duplicate it or not.

Judith told me Andrew would be my only student; the program would grow after people saw how successful our class was. I trusted her. I found it ironic that of all people, I (the child who hated school) would wind up being a teacher. But, it also made perfect sense, because I had always hoped someone would have taken the time to tailor my education to my individual needs.

As the year went on it did happen that more children joined our class. I would sometimes stand back that year teaching and wonder what anyone who walked in would think of the class. Children were all doing separate tasks; often I was overwhelmed but never lost my cool. It was a safe place where exploration was encouraged. Even a tantrum was good. It meant the child was trying to express him or herself. I did my best to be a calm, detached and loving observer. I knew I had to be.

2

It is an excruciatingly hot June day in 1979. My Mom pulls our yellow station wagon into a parking lot behind Macy's in downtown Morristown, New Jersey. She is handed a parking card and maneuvers into a spot as well as she can. My youngest brother, Timothy, is in a car seat in the front next to Sean the eldest, who is ten years old. My older sister, Barbara, is in the back next to my younger sister, Lizzie, and my older brother, Tucker. I am in the very back. We all pile out. As we pile out my mother pulls the stroller out of the trunk and puts Timothy into it. We are just like troops waiting for the General to give us the go ahead.

My mother is 8 months pregnant. "Let's go kids. We are here to buy Sean a bathing suit and nothing else. I don't want anyone asking me for things. We're here for your brother's bathing suit for swim team and THAT IS IT, understood?" No one objects; all five of us follow my mom.

We go in through Macy's back doors, take the elevator down to the first floor and walk out the front doors. We walk down the block a few stores from Macy's and enter a local children's specialty store. We have to help my mom down the stairs with the stroller because there is no elevator to the boys' section in the basement. Everyone is sweating. The heat is unbearable. You can hardly breathe until you enter the air-conditioned store. I can't imagine what my mother feels like. She is a petite 5' and she holds all of her pregnancy weight in her stomach. People stare at us wherever we go with disbelief and compassion.

Sean is in the racks of bathing suits.

"Mom, I want the small ones."

"Sean, I am not buying you the small ones, they're for the older boys on the team. You can get the longer shorts."

"Mom, but I WANT the smaller ones."

"I heard you say what you want. What you want and what you are going to get are two different things. I will not buy you those and that is final. I am not going to stand here and argue with you all day about this. Let's go."

We help my mom with the stroller up the steep stairs and to the front door of the store. Sean stays lingering, looking at the older boy bathing suits.

"Let's go kids, Sean will follow, just keep going. I know it's hot but we're leaving and you can go in the sprinkler when we get home."

As we walk out my mother checks to make sure Sean is following. Once we reach the parking lot, we stand outside the car. No sign of Sean anymore. My mom looks over her shoulder again. She waits a couple of minutes. We can't even wait in the car. The inside of the car is like a furnace and it's better to stand in the heat.

"Kids, let's walk back into Macy's, your brother is taking his time."

We all walk back into Macy's but there is no sign of Sean. We go down the elevator and out the front doors; still no Sean. He is lost. We retrace our paths for more than half an hour.

We are now in the "lost and found" department of Macy's. My mother explains to a customer service representative that her son is missing and she needs help from the police. A policeman shows up to speak with my mother.

"I'm sorry, ma'am, but it must be a full 24 hours until anything can be done."

"WHAT? You mean to tell me that you're not going to try and help me find my son?"

"The best we can tell you is to go home and wait."

"WAIT and go HOME? WHY would I go home if my son is clearly lost somewhere in this vicinity?"

"Mrs. Marshall, I'm sorry but we don't know if he is still in the vicinity. If a child is lost it is very common for him or her to go home."

"I live 15 minutes away, probably more than five miles, one town over. Are you suggesting that my son could somehow get from here to there on his own?"

"Mrs. Marshall, please, I can see that you are upset but it is really the only thing you can do at this point."

We stand there looking up and down the streets until my pregnant mother, out of sheer exhaustion, decides we will go home.

We silently pile into the car. None of us have said a word since the whole incident began. We know not to. Mom doesn't usually freak out like this.

As Mom drives down our development street she can see the backyard swing set. Sean is on it, sitting on a swing. She quickly pulls into our driveway with a sense of urgency and relief. We are all equally relieved to be home and glad that another one of Sean's escapades is over. We carry on with our usual routines and go in through the garage to the kitchen and immediately head to the freezer for an ice pop as if nothing out of the ordinary has gone on. As quickly as we grab them out of the freezer we run out the door to the backyard to set up the sprinkler.

My mother has just walked in the door with the baby. She puts the baby down and runs to the backyard. She hugs my brother and smacks his backside so hard that he leaps forward.

"Get inside, Sean. NOW!"

He walks through the kitchen and into the living room. He sits down on the piano bench with the piano to his back like an obedient child waiting for his punishment.

The oldest brother always stands out as an example of what you are and what you are not allowed to do. I didn't know how to feel about what Sean did that afternoon but I knew I felt sorrow for both of them. My mother screamed questions at him as he sat on the piano bench, smacking him and then hugging him. I quietly observed, trying to understand the mixed feelings of love and anger, hoping this would never happen to me.

3

It was late August of 1997 in Baltimore and the first day of school was approaching. I looked forward to learning about Andrew and helping him with his challenges. I knew he would say 2-3 word phrases if he was excited, but that was the extent of his verbal communication.

I didn't know what PDD was until I had met Andrew in Judith's home office. I was told by Judith that PDD is a form of autism, but I barely knew what autism was. I had never interacted with any autistic child. With my limited understanding of his difficulties and having observed him only once, I would teach him every day for the entire school year.

Andrew walked into my classroom that first day with his newly-cut brown hair, staring at the floor. He walked a few steps ahead of his mother who was excited about her son's first real day of school.

His mother was talking nervously as soon as she entered our temporary makeshift classroom. The state had not approved my classroom for the first day of school. We were waiting for the final safety inspection for the fire door, so instead we worked out of an empty classroom that was used as a computer room. I had rolled one of the shelves from the primary classroom into the temporary room along with a love seat couch so we had something comfortable to sit on. Surrounding us were many metal desks. They were piled high, and were too large for Andrew to sit at, so I left them pushed to the side. Instead, we used dividers that were against the wall to create some areas of clear space. Essentially, our classroom was the size of a walk-in closet but I knew it was only temporary. Given this backdrop, I concentrated on a gracious delivery as I introduced myself to Andrew and his mother. First, I interrupted his mother to refocus his attention.

"Hello, Andrew. I'm Miss Maureen."

He did not respond to his name and did not speak. He continued to stare at the floor. His mom stood there looking like she was feeling awkward and filled in any silence with conversation and prodding her son to speak. She knew her son didn't respond to people's questions and this was her way of dealing with her misfortune. I did not nor could I really understand how she must have felt as a parent of a child who barely spoke.

"Well, we are going to have fun today, Andrew, so why don't you tell your mom goodbye and we'll start our day."

I thought he wanted his mother to leave because he did what I asked. Most children his age would want their mother to stay. He kept his stare fixed on the gray tile floor and said a barely audible, "Bye," while throwing up one of his hands, awkwardly waving goodbye. His mother was hesitant to leave. So, as well as she could, she smiled and left us for the day.

Head down, he walked over to the wooden shelf filled with all different toys, without raising his head. He appeared to me to be in a constant state of anger and disturbed concentration because his face was all scrunched up as if he were a grumpy old man. He pulled a train from the shelf.

"Andrew must like trains."

I observed for a few minutes and then interjected, "Andrew is holding a train. Miss Maureen will take out the tracks so we can make a great big train track together."

I started putting the wooden tracks together and Andrew remained standing with his train; he soon decided to sit down on the cold tile where I was working away.

A few minutes later he put his train on the track I had made for him.

"Andrew is putting his train on the train track."

"He is pushing his train up the hill."

"He is pushing his train down the hill. The train is at the end of the track. Andrew needs to add some more tracks for his train."

Andrew was ready to communicate. He picked up a train track and added it on and pushed his train a few more inches. He then began adding on more tracks.

Just then, Judith came in to visit. She noticed that Andrew was happy at his task.

"Hello Andrew!"

Andrew did not look up. Andrew knew Dr. Judith very well. He had been seeing her for speech therapy for two years.

"Andrew, what a great train! Show Dr. Judith how you play with your trains on the track."

Andrew silently got up and threw the train across the room. He took the train tracks and started throwing them in different directions.

I stepped away so I wouldn't get hit. Judith was in the room so I was able to observe how she would handle this.

"Andrew is angry. Andrew needs to stop."

Andrew ignored her and continued throwing things and proceeded to pick up a chair, throw it over and push more of the tables and chairs in all different directions.

In a monotone and firm voice Judith said, "Andrew, you need to stop throwing the trains or Dr. Judith will have to stop you."

Andrew did not respond so she took Andrew's arm and held it still and removed the track from his hand. Children with PDD or autism resist any type of physical contact with another person. Most are ultra-sensitive to touch and feel that being touched is an encroachment on their world. But Andrew did not try to hit Judith; instead he stood there breathing quickly and heavily through his nose and staring with a mean, scrunched-up face at the ground.

"Andrew, this behavior is not allowed. Dr. Judith is sitting you on the floor and you have to sit and breathe and calm down. Dr. Judith and Miss Maureen know you are upset but you may not throw toys."

Andrew sat after Judith physically guided him to a sitting position. He started to calm and Dr. Judith left soon after. Reading was the best way I could think of to calm Andrew. I quickly pulled one of my classic books from the shelf. Andrew continued to look away, staring at the ground.

"It is reading time and Miss Maureen is going to read Andrew a book. The book is called *Corduroy*."

I sat as close to Andrew as I could without disturbing him and I began to read. Andrew slowly turned his head toward the book to see what it was about. Andrew was out of his "rut"; by now it was lunchtime.

"Miss Maureen is going to bring Andrew to the sink and show Andrew how we wash."

Dr. Judith had pointed out that many children with severe communication disorders have trouble performing basic tasks, such as washing their hands and brushing their teeth. From a speech-language pathologist/teacher point of view, if these children did not perform these tasks (which none of them did) then it was a priority for me to make sure we started from ground up no matter how elementary it may have seemed to an outsider.

Andrew obediently got up from reading the book and walked with me to the sink.

"Miss Maureen is turning the water on. The water is on. Miss Maureen is putting soap in Andrew's hands. Andrew needs to put his hands together and wash." Andrew did nothing.

"Miss Maureen is helping Andrew wash."

I took his hands and placed them together to start scrubbing. I guided his hands towards the flowing faucet. He held his hands almost limp as I did all the work for him.

"Andrew is finished scrubbing and washing his hands so Miss Maureen is turning off the water. Andrew needs to dry his hands. Miss Maureen is getting a paper towel to dry Andrew's hands. Andrew's hands are dry. We are finished." Andrew looked up at me with a quick glance.

"Thank you for letting Miss Maureen see your handsome eyes." The rest of the day went by smoothly. Andrew's mother was twenty minutes early. She clearly wanted to observe. I did my best to keep my comments short so that a daily teacher's conference would not become expected.

"How did he do today?"

"He did great." I purposely didn't mention his throwing trains. She was clearly thrilled. I was glad to see the day was over. I was unsure as to exactly what I was doing and how I was structuring my day. What I did know was that all children are naturally egotistical. By constantly stating Andrew's actions I was helping him to be present and conscious of himself and his surroundings. My dialogue served as a reminder to him, and helped him associate words with his actions. Ultimately, by constantly keeping him verbally present in his surroundings, I was encouraging him to stay present and not slip away into himself. After only two weeks of religiously speaking to him all day long, you could see a change in Andrew's reaction to the world around him. Andrew was allowing me to enter into his "world" through his now consistent subtle acknowledgement of me. He was "letting me in" and from there I was gently pulling him into my world, our world, the larger world outside. Evidence of this was the fact that he was raising his head up more and more. His head was starting to look out into the world because he was beginning to want to see what it had to offer him; to see what was beyond the floor in front of his tiny feet.

Would I know what to do if he did in fact keep progressing? The fact of the matter was I didn't have any rule book telling me how to determine the "right" next goal once he met what seemed to be more obvious ones. There was no reference point for a measurable comparison because this was the first early intervention program that was ever run like this. My classroom did not function like a public school, from what I heard. Children with severe communication disorders have difficulty transitioning from one task to another. Public schools often addressed this issue by using Velcro symbols that were stuck to a board as a way to help the children understand that they were changing tasks. I had been told about these Velcro transition cards and even had made some, but I never did use them; I would use speech only. Our goal was to talk these children into "coming out into the world." Symbols would not be used. Speech would be the way we made our connection.

Each time Andrew progressed from our dialogue (despite the nonexistent rule book) we worked on the next piece of communication that was most crucial. The next most crucial tool for him was to stop looking at the floor and take in his surroundings and be present. Therefore, the next goal was to look at Ms. Maureen when saying "good morning." He started out with quick glances and his glances developed into eye contact. Once his eye contact was satisfactory, the language was built upon. Once the language was built upon, gestures and interaction were worked upon. I didn't know it at the time, but Judith hadn't given me a rule book because there wasn't one. No child responds the same way. Therefore, the most crucial thing would be understanding what Andrew's individual needs were, what his sensitivities and fears were and then from there, my interaction, instincts, and common sense would determine if this program would be a success in getting through to Andrew. This intense one-on-one teaching lasted for about three weeks. His tantrums had stopped and his eye contact had improved significantly. We still did not have a classroom but this was not prohibiting Andrew from progressing. I had tapped into Andrew's major communication barriers. I felt as if I was walking on a tightrope as I taught Andrew each day, but I also knew the rope was getting stronger each week. The tightening being that Andrew's behavior had become consistent. As a result of this intense therapy, Andrew was progressing at a rate that he had never experienced before. His mother had become calmer and as a result their resistance toward one another was decreasing noticeably. Dr. Judith was proving her early intervention concept right. I was not fully conscious of how great his improvements were because of the mere fact that I was so caught up in meeting his needs. This forced me to look to Judith for my objectivity concerning progress.

When I did have a moment for my own needs and thoughts, I was distracted by my fears. Fear of my own ignorance and of the possibility that I might do something wrong and not improve Andrew's life or any future students, for that matter. I would console myself by the thought that Judith would guide me. She would pass by and wave or just walk in the door for a few minutes and say one of her enthusiastic statements assuring me that everything was going great. I reasoned that she had been in the business for so long that it really only took her moments to assess the progress of my children. I trusted and hoped that this was the case. I knew I related to these children's sensitivities and fears but whether or not teaching using Judith's speech strategy and my own gut instincts would be enough worried me. Ironically, these children didn't seem so severe to me. If anything they appeared more scared and uncertain, but not unreachable. Something inside me told me I could do it, that I understood these children and this motivated me. So, I put my needs aside.

4

I grew up in the suburbs of Morris Plains, New Jersey, in a white five-bedroom split level style home with three floors. My morning routine was normal for me, but for those who didn't grow up with more than 5 other siblings, they were probably anything but ordinary.

"Maureen, it's 6:30 A.M., time to get up. You have school today."

If I don't respond she will think I am in a deep sleep. I pretend to be asleep whenever my mother wants me to do something. One time I was holding my brother's bottle for him while he sat in his baby seat on the floor. I was sick of doing it, so I just laid myself right down next to him while holding the bottle to his mouth and pretended I was sleeping. Who could sleep like that? While holding a bottle and lying on that cold ceramic floor? Certainly not me, but my mom thought I was sleeping. She thought it was cute so she took a picture. We still have it.

My dad used to call me "possum" because he would catch me opening one eye sometimes. I just denied it. Stick with the same story and your parents can't usually do much. Other times I would open up my eyes and just laugh because I was "caught" by my dad. It was peaceful to sleep; no one bothered me or asked me to do anything. I shut everything out. I would do this so I wouldn't have to interact with them. I liked people to be around but when there were too many people for me to handle at once, my way of coping was to be a possum.

"Maureen, I told you a half an hour ago and you're still not up! It's 7:00 A.M. now and the carpool will be here in 15 minutes. Now come on, get up!"

"I don't want to go to school, Mom. I'm tired. I don't feel well."

"What's wrong with you? You're not really sick. You have to go to school."

My mother was always easy when it came to staying home. She would offer us a "mental day" off from school. She always said that if you want to take a day off it might as well be when you are a kid because when you're an adult, you just can't take days off. Initially, she usually gave us a little bit of a challenge about staying home, but she never really stuck to her "tough" act.

Uggh, I would pull myself out of bed. I hated the morning. I was always so tired. The brightness of the early morning stung my eyes and they would fill up with tears, so I squinted until my eyes would adjust. I didn't want to go to school because most of all I dreaded the thought of someone telling me what to do all day long. Didn't anyone else see what I experienced every day as ridiculous? I didn't have an interest in sitting at a desk, trying to understand and process what the teachers wanted of me.

I quickly buttoned my yellow cotton/polyester blouse with half moon collars on it and pulled my green and navy plaid jumper over my head. I always had my uniform resting on the end of my bed before I went to sleep every night. The nuns would get mad if I forgot my navy knee-highs and it was nearly impossible to find matching navy socks in the amount of laundry that our family had. Does anyone know how many different shades of navy there are? My mom even tried to put a "sock system" into place so that we couldn't mix them up too much. Mom always tried very hard. Her system was a chart hanging on the laundry room wall. Next to each child's name was their designated color. That color was sewn into each pair of socks that you owned. The system didn't work. It just pissed me off more because it lowered my odds of finding another sock to match.

With my uniform on and somewhat functioning, I headed down the stairs. My bare feet touched the brown tile basement floor and I maneuvered my way past the ironing board reaching the obstacle course of 8 or 10 baskets overflowing with clean clothes sitting on the floor in front of the folding table. The trick was getting to that table. Well, most people would call it a folding table, but we didn't have time for folding, so instead the laundry was taken out of the dryer and put on the table and when Mom had time she would throw each unfolded piece of clean laundry into each person's designated basket. My coordination was nonexistent at 7 A.M., so instead of the possibility of scraping my legs by walking in between the bins of clothing, I stepped on top of each bin, like playing leapfrog on Atari. I quickly made my way to the table edge balancing myself on the clean bin of clothes beneath my feet. The laundry on the table reached higher than my head and it was heavy. I threw the "big" pieces of clothing to the corners and dug below for socks. I was playing the sock lottery. As I reached under the mound of clothes I hoped my hands would find the navy knee-highs. No such luck, I had Dad's black business socks in my right hand. Actually, no that was my left hand. My insurance policy for knowing the difference between my left and right was that my left hand finger always had a callus on it where I tightly gripped my pencil from the stress of the school day. Come on navy knee-highs, Mrs. Smith will be here soon! I pull out my other hand from beneath the clothes. I now have Anne's little girl pink frilly socks. Not what I need, but they would be fun to wear. I should have done this last night.

"Maureen, let's go, they will be here any minute!"

Never out loud, but in my head I thought, Damn it, I know but I only have one blue sock, just a few more minutes. Oh, and today.... Oh yeah, it's Monday. I have gym. Gym meant that I wouldn't be held captive to our one classroom, but also that I would have to hope my navy gym shorts and powder blue gym top were in my laundry bin. If not, I could steal Lizzie's from her bin. I'm way too tired for all of this right now. OK, keep going. I have to find my white socks too or the gym teacher will get mad. Why do so many people care what color your stupid socks are? I longed to go to a different school and to have an easier life.

From downstairs in our yellow tiled kitchen my mother yelled, "Maureen Rose! Mrs. Smith is here!" My siblings would go running out the door as they grabbed their brown-bagged lunches with their names on it. I continued my internal dialogue, *Blue socks and gym clothes are going to have to be it for the day with no white socks. I'll just have to get a pink slip. That's just great, I already know I am getting one pink slip for the day and if I get two more I'll have detention. Great, more time spent at school. I don't want to go.*

"Maureen, NOW!"

I couldn't stand carpooling. It was usually Mrs. Smith who picked us up in her white caravan with brown paneling. I was always the last one in the van. Sometimes they would honk the horn because I was so late. I didn't care. I wished they would leave. I didn't want to go to school anyway, especially not in that crowded car; it was claustrophobic. I always got the worst seat in the van. The first thing I would notice were the smells from the soaps and shampoos that everyone had used that morning. Mrs. Smith was different from any mom I was used to. Her perfume was always so strong. I don't even know if my mom owned perfume. She would do her nails while driving the car and the smell of the polish would fill the entire car. Until this day, I have never seen nail polish on my mother. To top the entire situation off was the music. Mrs. Smith chose the music in the car and it was always some cheesy soft rock that would make you want to jump out of the car. I think my mom was just happy we were all in the car and let us play whatever we wanted. Thank God there was only one more stop and then we were at school. She dropped us off in the parking lot. I had one of the longest walks down the hallway because I was in the lower grades.

For some reason, everything from the carpool to just getting to the classroom each morning seemed like a chore that I didn't want to do. I knew I had to do what everyone told me but I didn't like the feeling that someone controlled everything I did. I felt like I wasn't being treated as a competent person and I turned inward. So much seemed repetitive and not enjoyable. I felt like I was watching scenes unfold around me all day long. Most words I wasn't interested in even trying to process because I was more concerned with observing the actions and pictures that formed before me than anything else. Consequently, art class was my favorite. We had it once a week and I was good at it. Pictures were my language. I didn't have any type of explanation for why this was the case until I was diagnosed with a learning disability in my later school years. I didn't really know what to make of being labeled "learning disabled" other than the fact that something wasn't right with me. So, I kept quiet, kept my internal complaints to myself, and every day at school I went to the same wooden heavy double door closets that made a huge clank when you open and shut them. I hung my book bag on my hook, and then sat down at my desk. We were told to stand and immediately I looked at my surroundings as I placed my right hand over my heart.

"I pledge allegiance to the flag...."

(Alison's not here today. She's always the best at jump roping at snack. It's not going to be as fun without her.)

"one nation..."

(We have Religion after this, maybe Sister will be sick today. Then we could have an extra long recess.)

"...justice for all."

I memorized by listening to the melody, not the words. Muffled sounds were all I could hear after the first few words of the pledge. So, I stood and did as I was told while I let my eyes take in the pictures of life surrounding me. I'm sure the fact that I felt exhausted every morning contributed to my inability to focus on words. I now know that I had a slight auditory processing problem. Almost every autistic child and a large number of learning disabled children have this problem as well. In plain terms, my brain could not process the words that people said to me as quickly as a "normal" person processes sounds and words. I never realized that this was why I always said, "What?" after someone asked a question even though I knew I had heard what they said. By the time I finished saying, "What?" I had processed what was said to me and had answered the person. Sometimes all I heard were jumbled sounds that didn't create whole words. This is especially true when I would listen to music. The words were often said so rapidly that I had no idea what was being sung. It was not until my twenties that I really began to hear words within music. If I did know the words of a song it was only when the pronunciation was very clear or I could read the lyrics. I loved *The Sound of Music* soundtrack when I was a kid. The lyrics are very clear and simple. We also had the sheet music. I read the words and memorized them. I would tape myself singing and hum those words all day.

Holding the flag every once in a while or putting the number on the calendar were the two things in our morning routine that I liked doing; at least it was different than the equivalent of sleeping while standing up and reciting things. I had an obsession with the calendar. I wanted all 30 or 31 numbers to be up. I would stare at the calendar during the school day and count how many days were left in order to complete the month. If we were at the beginning of the month I couldn't wait until we got to the end of the week so at least an entire line would be in order. I can't explain this urge; it was just a picture in my head that I constantly wanted "fixed." Maybe it was because I was confused by my surroundings and therefore became obsessive about the visual order of things.

Once our morning rituals were completed, our official school day would begin. We would sit down at our desks and Sister Gretchen would come in for our religion class. She was a large lady, rectangular in shape and very rigid looking.

Sr. Gretchen's face wasn't very appealing to look at, so I didn't. Instead, I looked at the boy who sat diagonally across from me. His name was Bigsby. He was albino and he always looked sad. I felt badly for him. While in school I don't remember ever listening to any teacher for more than a few minutes. After a few words I would "zone out" and my thoughts would go to different things or dialogues. Most consistently, it was hunches about the people, the environment or desks that I observed. I would stare at the grain of my desk and look at the pattern of the wood. Then with my pencil I would follow the pattern when no one was looking and erase it quickly so I wouldn't get in trouble. I was frequently mesmerized by patterns, colors, and staying within lines.

I'll never forget how Bigsby would sit staring. That's what I felt like doing. He was like me. I remember his last day in first grade.

Sr. Gretchen was speaking about the usual important Catholic school topics.

"You must all thank God for Jesus' sacrifice of dying on the cross for us. It was the ultimate act of unselfishness and love for us. I have a worksheet today with Jesus, I want you to use your best coloring skills and make these cheery so that we can hang them in the hall for parents' night."

We took our crayons out from our desks and began our assignment. I was always happy to color. I was good at it. I even won coloring contests when I got older. I remember looking over at Bigsby coloring his picture, making it entirely black with his crayon. I kept looking over. No, his Jesus wasn't African American; he was nonexistent. You couldn't even see the lines where Jesus was anymore. It was just one big black blob. I was sad for Bigsby. Life was hard for him and the only way he could express his hardship was through that black crayon. Wait till the teacher sees this. Oh, here we go....

"Bigsby, what is this? Is this the assignment I just gave you?" He didn't even look up at Sister Gretchen.

"This is a disgrace; you are going to have to go see Principal Margaret."

I worried about Bigsby and wondered what was wrong with the teacher. Why was she yelling at him when he was clearly sad? I mean, if I started coloring everything black, I hope my mother wouldn't yell at me. I would hope she would say, "What is wrong honey?" Not, "Go to your room." Why doesn't she get that children don't try to be bad for no reason? Bigsby never returned to school after that day.

Despite my lack of interest and frustrations, for the most part, I did like first grade. My teacher, Ms. Lepson, was a young, pretty lady who was family friends with my mother and had been taught by my mom when she was a little girl. She seemed like she would be nice so I decided I might like her.

As I packed up to leave for the end of the day, Ms. Lepson called on me.

"Maureen, can you come up to my desk when you are done packing your bag?"

"Yes, Ms. Lepson."

"Your grandfather will be picking you up from school today. Your mother went to the hospital this afternoon in labor. I can't wait to hear if you have a new little sister or brother."

I smiled and went back to my desk.

As I walked out to the parking lot I saw my big-bellied grandfather waiting by his car for us to come out of school.

I said, "Hi Grandpa," as I gave him a kiss on the cheek.

"Hi pumpkin. Your mom is at the hospital in labor so I have carpool duty today." I smiled again and started to get into the perfectly kept brown, 1970's Cadillac.

"Wait, Maureen, let's put your bag in the trunk."

Grandpa was always a quiet man so we rode in silence except for the occasional noise or comment that my siblings would make.

As we pulled into the driveway we all hopped out and entered the kitchen where Grandma had snacks for us.

"Everyone first change out of your uniforms, wash up and then come back downstairs for a snack."

These orders were completely uncharacteristic but we all did as we were told. After all, we were used to our independence when at home. There simply were no rules having to do with daily routines. Grandma stayed over that night and Grandpa went home to their place. As it got late I realized my Grandpa had left with my book bag in his trunk.

I went into school the next morning with the good news that I had a new little sister, Anne, and what I thought was a very good excuse as to why I didn't have my homework assignment done.

Miss Lepson gave me a pink slip. I was angry and felt that she should have taken my situation into consideration. Didn't she understand the challenges I endured every day? Why would she turn on me like this when she had seemed like someone who really wanted to help me? Clearly, she did not understand me and was just another person I would shut out like the rest of the world.

She was another adult who couldn't see that my inability to understand my school environment, which was overly structured, created a lack of excitement and peacefulness. Consequently, I was always relieved to go home from school because I wanted to get out of the place that didn't feed my interests. However, once I got home, I would become overwhelmed by witnessing so many different needs, conflicts and emotions (which any family as large as ours would have on a daily basis) and this generated more questioning within. Experiencing so many emotions that I couldn't understand on a daily basis at school and home compounded the confusion of my internal thoughts, causing me to turn to silence more frequently. I would then turn to my youngest siblings for peacefulness. I would play with whichever baby at the time needed comforting and found a feeling of content and belonging. For some reason, my experiences were exhausting me and I couldn't explain why.

More importantly, thank God Mom had finally had Anne when she did because I was getting worried her belly would explode. I really thought she might go into labor the other night when Sean threw a whole plate of spaghetti over her head. My grandmother was over helping out because she could tell my mother was going to have the baby any day. Grandma must have been horrified by what she saw and my mother must have been deeply embarrassed. Sean really was in a vicious cycle that he didn't know how to stop. My mother didn't know how to help him out of it either. Understandably so, Mom was regularly overwhelmed by the needs of so many. Consequently, there was a lack of individual attention and structure in our everyday lives and Sean dealt with this by rebelling.

5

It had been about four weeks when we were finally approved by the state to use our classroom, and it seemed large for just the two of us, but this changed shortly after our move. About a week later the principal popped her head in while Andrew and I were sitting on the carpet.

"Hello Miss Maureen and Andrew."

I prompted Andrew to say hello and he did.

"Can I borrow your ear for a second Miss Maureen?"

"Yes, of course." I quickly got up from the carpet and stepped into the hallway, watching Andrew from the door.

"I just wanted to let you know that I spoke with Judith about a little boy whose mother works in the office. She needs him looked after while she works and we thought it would be a nice addition to the classroom."

"That sounds great."

"Good, Simon will start tomorrow."

"OK, thanks."

I was happy to hear that Andrew would have another child to play with.

The next morning, at the start of the day, Simon was dropped off at my classroom. Simon, who was a "normal" child of 6 years old, showed resistance when being left by his mother. His mother stayed for 15 minutes and pulled herself away from his tight grasp as she assured him that she would be right down the hall.

He was fine soon after she left. He was a sweet boy who was significantly taller than Andrew. He played well with Andrew that first day as he suspiciously observed my speaking style prompting Andrew to recognize and include Simon in his play. My constant verbalizations were foreign to him but by the end of the day it was as if he didn't know any different.

Simon settled in quickly. He obviously had more developed communication skills and this was an extremely good thing for Andrew. It would serve as an example of how he could develop and use these skills himself. Just as all children do, they had disagreements but it was always something that could be handled quite easily and they learned from one another. Later, when more children joined our class, Simon became friends with all his challenged classmates. He was a good kid who benefited from his peers as much as they did from him.

He also dealt with some difficult situations and became a more patient and understanding little boy. Quite frankly, sometimes it was just amusing to see how a "normal" child handled the abnormal occurrences we had. For example, one of his classmates might be standing right next to him playing and then just bolt out of the classroom; another who appeared to be calmly playing might all of a sudden scream; another might not respond to the question he had repeated three times. Instead of getting frustrated, he would just figure out another way to either communicate or would simply start a different task. As a child, he obviously didn't realize the unusual adjustments he was making but an outsider may have seen humor in his compromises. Despite the fact that he was unimpaired, it was still another dynamic that I had to consider in my daily tasks.

Once again, Andrew adjusted to our new situation and before long it seemed that Simon had always been there. The classroom really did feel like a "normal" one with minimal focus on any communication impairments. Both boys continued making progress as I methodically spoke to them describing what they were doing and stating what their actions meant just as Judith had taught me. Much like Andrew, Simon's improvements came quickly. Simon's shyness and whining had disappeared. He became more confident in stating what he needed and asked questions. I wondered if there really was any difference in the emotional needs of these two boys despite the fact that from a clinical standpoint they would be considered very different.

I never knew when I would see Judith because she had a different schedule each day. When I did see her, I was relieved and communicated my uncertainty as to what I should do for projects. She said she had a book of exercises that she would give me. Shortly after, Judith gave me that binder which consisted of letter and sound worksheets with simple cut, color and paste exercises. I began to do one of those worksheets each day. I felt temporary relief having at least one project I knew we could do. The rest of the day was guided playtime with snack, lunch and hygiene routines. I felt something was missing from our days but this was the best I knew how to do so I made the rest up as we went. No one was saying anything was wrong, so with a guilty uncertainty I continued doing only what I knew best.

At this point I could feel that my children's hearts trusted mine and we were becoming a team. A team that was learning to embrace the world outside of itself. I accomplished this by working from my heart, not from a clinical standpoint, even though I knew this was what I was supposed to be attempting to do. Two of only a few consistent things that year were the sound of my non-stop descriptive voice and my heartfelt compassion for what these children felt inside. Whether this approach would be successful was still unknown, but if the children's progress were an indicator, things were going well.

Speaking non-stop all day long was difficult for me. I had always been the quiet one. Consequently, I typically ended my day completely drained.

I didn't recognize it at the time, but I was also learning a great deal and this was another factor that required an extreme amount of energy. I was learning to be a teacher, a speech therapist and most of all how to communicate on the children's terms. One of my most reliable resources for teaching guidelines was my own experience as a student. I knew that the most exhausting thing for me when I was a child in the classroom was a lack of stimulation and excitement. So, I knew that if I was bored, there was a 99% chance my kids were bored, too. I would not let the exhaustion that boredom could bring pass onto them. I knew that boredom could easily throw them back into their muted internal world.

6

I stood with my head tilted back with one hand holding the tissue to my nose and the other hand applying pressure while squeezing the ridge of my nose. This was the position my mother and doctor had told me to stand in more times than I could count. The bleeding was sure to stop then. All I could concentrate on was the feeling of the warm blood cascading down my throat. I hated that taste. I never questioned my mother for an explanation as to why I had those nosebleeds that lasted for a minimum of thirty minutes, day after day after day. I couldn't even pass my hand by my nose without worrying that it would start up again. I didn't really know anything different. Life went on and I had to get to school. So, with my tissue in hand and my head cocked back, off I went. I knew it would eventually stop. I would do the "test": I would dab the front of my nose to see if the red dot of blood had decreased enough so at least I could stop holding my head back. By the time we got to the school parking lot I was sitting with my head up and a wad of tissues in hand. I would survive, I always did. I was in third grade then.

My third grade teacher was Sister Penelope but we called her Sister Pencil. She was thin and very strict. Sr. Pencil always wore the same white nun outfit, a long white skirt past her knee with a white habit on her head.

She talked too quickly, in short sentences. She was plain looking with short brownish-red hair. Her hair was a little bit like Julie Andrews in *The Sound of Music*. The difference was that I liked Julie Andrews.

Third grade was not a source of satisfaction for me so I focused on trying to "make this world a better place" like my mom told me. This world didn't seem so great. The best I could do was to help out with my siblings and be nice to everyone. I would rather not say anything than chat about something without substance, so I mostly just said hello and smiled.

I sat in the front seat, center row. I hated it because the teacher could see me well and would call on me a lot. I preferred the back where no one would bother me and I didn't have to look like I was paying attention. Sitting in the front made me nervous for various reasons. Most of all, I felt self-conscious in front of my peers, because it seemed I couldn't find the fun they could find while at school. I didn't know what to talk about that was of substance and because of this fact, I wondered if they viewed me as strange. I also never knew what Sr. Pencil was saying and I wouldn't know the answer if she asked me a question.

She would tell me I wasn't listening and then yell at me in front of everyone. The chalkboard became more and more difficult for me to see; squinting was not working anymore.

"Maureen, can you please read the next question and answer it for me?"

"Yes, Sister."

I paused for a minute because I couldn't remember which question we were on. I didn't know because I was still trying to understand the answer that was given for number one.

"Maureen, number 3, please read it out loud!"

"What is the name of the verb in the last sentence in the paragraph above?"

I paused for a second or two, which seemed like an eternity. I started to get very nervous and I forgot what I just read. I have to read it again to myself quickly but she is waiting for an answer.

"Maureen, what is the verb?"

I repeated her question in my head again, *What is the verb? Verb.....a verb is an action word.*

"Maureen, look at sentence number three."

"I'm looking at sentence number three."

"Read it again to yourself, Maureen."

I wish she would stop talking so I can concentrate.

"Maureen, are you listening?"

"Yes, Sister." My body temperature was starting to rise.

"Well, what is the verb?"

I am already uncomfortable and distracted by the fact that my body doesn't feel right.

I repeat the sentence to myself, "The man is feeling very ill; he is nauseous."

Sister is still waiting along with the other 16 kids in my class. Is "is" a part of the verb...? I finally give up; it's better to say nothing than get it wrong.

I say very quietly, "I'm not sure, Sister."

I want to cry because I feel incompetent. I can't think straight at all. I start to pray, "Please, let her have someone else answer the question so this can end."

"Can someone help Maureen out and answer the question?" Doesn't she know that I don't want any help; I just don't want this pressure.

"Erin?"

It's over. I hate Sr. Pencil for asking me questions.

I forget to listen to the answer. I can't find what question they are on again. I look across the aisle and see what Danny is doing. He is writing the answer to number 6 but I missed the answers to 4 and 5. At least I know the number they are on if she calls on me again but now I missed the answer to 6! <u>Focus, Maureen.</u>

"Joey was walking the dog."

"The verb is *was walking*."

"Put your English workbooks in your desk and grab your snacks, we will have snack time outside today." It's not even lunchtime yet. I am ready to go to sleep. I ask to be excused to the girls room before I get my snack. I walk into the stall and as I pull up my jumper I realize I still have my pink strawberry shortcake pajamas on under my skirt. I was so out of it that morning that I pulled my jumper over my head and forgot to pull my pajama bottoms off. I'm embarrassed enough from English and now I feel mortified. How am I going to get them off with no one knowing? I want to go home. When I go back into the classroom everyone is out on the lawn for recess. I go to my backpack in the closet for my snack, close the closet door behind me for privacy and slip my pink shorts off. Whew, problem solved.

Sr. Pencil finally changed our seats at Thanksgiving. I was in the center row but 3 seats back. I would rather be in the far right corner by the windows, but it was an improvement. The only problem now was that I couldn't see her thin, long cursive penmanship on the blackboard. At first I didn't say anything to my mom because she was so busy and I knew the eye doctor was expensive. My mom always said that all doctors were expensive. I finally decided I would have to tell her I couldn't see. She laughed at me but eventually took me to the eye doctor. My mom thought I was lying but I was right. Now I looked more like my mom. I had jet-black short hair with my huge eyes. My glasses were the pearly yellowish kind and looked like mini Mom glasses. At least I could see the board. Now maybe Mom would finally let me grow my hair out so I wouldn't look too nerdy. She always told my sister Lizzie and me that she could see our pretty faces better if we had short hair. I really wanted to grow my hair out. With long hair, I could pull it away from my face.

As Lizzie and I got under our white and red matching floral comforters that night my mother opened the door and peeked her head in. She would often see red cardboard bricks dividing the room evenly in half. My apparent neurotic tendency to insist on visual order was the cause of this division. Lizzie was not someone who cared for visual order and I was a neat freak. I couldn't stand the disorder and the way I dealt with it (after I had complained to her enough and she wouldn't clean it up) would be to literally divide the room up with our cardboard bricks. I felt most at peace knowing that her stuff was on her disheveled side of the room while mine was spotless and tidy.

"Thank God for everything and ask him to help you always be good girls and always do what's right, Amen."

"Amen."

We said that same prayer every night. I thanked God every single night for each of my siblings. I felt I had to protect them so I would go through each and every one of their names and ask God to keep them safe because I could not bear it if one were hurt. I knew I was blessed that all my siblings were healthy and safe, but I didn't understand why every day was so difficult and why I didn't feel like I belonged.

7

Jonas was a handsome brown-haired, brown-eyed charming little fellow. He had a severe to profound language disorder classified as dysarthria and apraxia. Dysarthria is characterized by incoordination of speech muscles. Apraxia is the inability of the oral muscles to communicate properly with the brain. He also had a "global language disorder" which means it affected his reading, writing, speaking, and listening. Like Andrew, he also came into my class unable to make eye contact, looking down toward the floor only.

Jonas sprinted into the classroom and made a loud screeching noise indicating that he was excited. I quickly learned that sprinting was a favorite habit of his. He ran to the oversized waffle blocks and quickly started to put them together in a very out of control manner.

His mother, Leslie, an Orthodox Jewish woman, was dressed in a long flowing skirt and oversized cotton shirt.

She smiled and looked down as if embarrassed for her son's behavior and shyly said, "He's excited."

I smiled and said, "That's great, we are excited to have Jonas here too."

"Well, then I will see you at 2:30 to pick Jonas up?"

"Great."

Jonas had a pale complexion with black thick wavy hair. He was adorably disheveled. He made quick uncontrollable movements throughout the day. He could not calm down unless doing his preferred tasks. All of these tasks involved building. Using a hammer was his favorite activity. It seemed to me he was letting out aggression. Many times I would go home with bruises from him. He would kick and not realize he was kicking someone.

He had limited bodily control. His posture was very extreme. At one moment his shoulders were very erect, like that of a soldier, and at another moment he would completely round his shoulders. Somehow his bottom torso always balanced him out. It was like looking at one of those dolls that is made up of a string and attached to a platform. When you pull that string taut, the entire doll stands up straight and stiff as a soldier. If you let go the doll just falls in all different directions. This was Jonas.

I believe I understood Jonas more than most. He was one of six children. I knew the over-stimulation and chaos that he was inevitably exposed to by living with so many people. I also understood his desire to bolt. After all, there were many days I dreamed of running away from my own situations but simply didn't out of fear.

Jonas vocalized with jumbled words that he would shout out. He would yell them out randomly, in either a very high pitched voice or an extremely low tone. Thank goodness there was no classroom directly across from us.

I walked over and approached Jonas. He didn't indicate that he noticed anyone was there. I said his name.

"Hi Jonas! Wow, Jonas is so happy and excited to play with the blocks. Jonas is doing a great job." He glanced over quickly and looked away.

"Jonas really likes to build." He screeched again.

"Miss Maureen is going to ask Andrew if he would like to play with the blocks, too." I walked over to Andrew, who would now look up whenever I called his name.

"Andrew, let's play blocks with our new friend, Jonas."

Andrew got up from the carpet and walked over to the blocks. Jonas had a play hammer in his hand and was banging it. Then, he began moving around the blocks. I had picked up the rest of our play tools and brought them over to Jonas and Andrew.

I said, "Miss Maureen has tools." Jonas stopped and looked over at my hands. He rushed over and grabbed the tool out of my hand.

"Jonas took the tools from Miss Maureen's hands. Jonas needs to ask Miss Maureen for the tools." Jonas glanced over quickly again.

Andrew was busy at work on the other side of the creation. Jonas used his body so much for every task that he constantly dropped his yarmulke, otherwise referred to by him as his "Kippah," which was one word of only a few in his vocabulary. Throughout the day, he would occasionally notice that he had dropped it from his head and would yell, "Kippah, Kippah!"

Jonas was looking for something new to use in his creation so he scampered over to grab what he saw in my other hand and screeched.

I responded, "Jonas wants the tool. Jonas needs to say 'Tool please.'"

He said, in a very quick and low tone, "Tool."

"Thank you, Jonas, you asked for the tool. You may have the tool." He snatched it quickly as I held it out. We played with those tools EVERY day because they created motivation and desire in him like no other. It was a motivation I felt devoid of as a child when it came to school.

8

As the year progressed, we started learning more traditional subjects from Sister Pencil. My ability to keep up with what was going on in the classroom was becoming more difficult. Everything appeared to be performed at a very fast pace and I almost never had any interest in what was going on.

As I sat on my older sister's bedroom floor, my back against the closet doors, my mom and sister sat beside me.

"I just don't get it, Mom," I said, nearly in tears.

"Honey, it's a times table. It is actually a very logical thing. Think about this, if you have 2 of something and you need that something for 4 people, how many do you need? You would need 8 because 2 for each person would add up to eight. So, you get the times table 2 X 4 (the people) = 8."

"Mom, I just don't understand how they came up with the numbers, I don't think that way."

My oldest sister, Barbara, then stepped in for another crack at helping me to understand. I knew her intentions were good but it wasn't worth it. Instead, it was two people speaking two different languages to me rather than just one.

The exhaustion I experienced from trying to keep up with the school day resulted in my brain shutting down by the time I got home. I was so tired that nothing made sense to me. I knew I would just have to memorize the tables without understanding them. I survived all of my school experience by memorizing words and numbers without meaning. I recall one day Barbara telling me that I had an extremely good memory. I had no idea that my memory was considered good. I didn't seem to think anything in my brain was good. It was always lacking and I was practicing what I thought were purely survival tactics.

As I sat on the chaise lounge staring at the TV, my sister Lizzie sat on the dark brown floral couch that matched the dreariness of the rust-colored shaggy rug. I sat in my chair agitated with thoughts of anxiety from the day and methodically pulled out my eyelashes one by one, each time wishing for something that would bring me temporary happiness. I was sometimes compulsive, but mostly I just internally questioned everything and why life seemed so hard. I had heard from someone that whenever an eyelash falls out you make a wish and it comes true. I decided I wasn't going to wait for them to fall out. I was in a more urgent state of need. I wanted the dream Barbie dollhouse like my friend, Sally, but it was expensive and my mom did not like Barbies and the message they gave to her daughters. This was the best way I could think of getting that dollhouse. I put my thumb and index finger to my eyelashes and pulled. I got two at a time for that pull, but it pinched! I could do it; it was only temporarily painful. I pulled each and every one of my eyelashes out that day, and each and every eyelash was used for the same wish — the Barbie dream house.

As I walked upstairs when my mother called for dinner, she looked at my huge hazel, almond-shaped eyes and said, "What did you do?" I hesitated.

As I looked down at the floor I said, "I was making wishes."
She said, "WHAT?"
Mumbling I said, "I was making wishes with my eyelashes."
"You don't pull your eyelashes out to make wishes! I hope they grow back! Why would you do that to your beautiful eyes?"
"I was just making wishes."
"Sit down and eat your dinner."

I never told my mother until years later what my wishes were for because she never asked. I think I would have had that Barbie dream house if I had told her.

It was now summer and I was watching one of my younger siblings, which I often did because I enjoyed it. I was good at it and it created meaning for me.

"Good job, Annie. You can do it. One more step." My little sister is going to lose her footing. "Woops, there she goes..."

"Look, Anne, it's OK, no blood."

Anne Marie was a beautiful little dirty blonde-haired girl just about a year old and she was trying to master the stairs. She started crying like any normal one-year-old would after falling down. Anne sat on my lap as I distracted her from her pain.

"Let me see, does it move?" I bend Anne's leg back and forth to show her that her knee and leg still work.

"You are fine; I know it scared you. Let's get you a band-aid to make it all better." Annie stares up with her wide eyes into mine as if she knows she can trust me and stops crying.

I noticed my mom had walked up and observed me taking care of Anne. She sat down next to us on the once-baby-blue carpeted stairs that were now worn gray from being stepped on by all seven kids, and gave me a kiss on my forehead.

As I look up she turns to me and says, "Maureen, I love you. Just remember, you are here to make the world a better place, that's the most important thing, OK?"

I didn't especially want that responsibility. I wanted to be a kid. I just wanted to play with my dolls, play teacher, play movie star, or anything I felt like. Like any child, I played because it took me out of the present world and into my own world of peace. She hugged me saying, "I love you."

I gave her a hug in return and pulled away so I could go play. I determined that it was a long enough hug.

"OK, Mom. Can I stop watching the baby now and go outside?" My mom just smiles and kisses me again. I ran toward our kitchen door to the backyard before she could say another word to me.

As I raced out the door I grabbed my baby doll and spoke quietly to her, "OK, Jennifer, little doll baby, we will go outside and have a picnic on a blanket and then go for a walk in the stroller." I loved my dolls so much; I would protect them from everything.

I wanted to have the picnic but couldn't stop the constant dialogue going on in my head. I was thinking about what my mom had just said to me. I felt the responsibility to nurture my siblings as if they were my dolls. I had the ability to observe their actions and seemed to understand the type of love they needed. I was a mother figure to them and didn't know it because I was simply doing what felt natural to me.

My sister is near my spot on the lawn. "Lizzie, do you want to come too?"

"Okay, let me go get my doll."

Lizzie is 6 years old and the same height as me. She is tall for her age and looks like a string bean with brown short wavy hair. She is naturally pretty and a perfect shade of brown from the sun. She is the more athletic of the two of us.

"Let's go over here where it is quiet, it's close to the swings."

I loved our swing-set. It was all silver metal with a really shiny slide. The monkey bars were my favorite. I loved stretching my arms as I hung, and when I was tired of hanging, I could swing right onto the slide to safety.

We decided to put our blanket (an old white comforter of my mom's) on a patch of grass that was burnt and brittle from the heat of the sun. There were no words to say; it was peaceful compared to the inside of my house. I didn't even mind if the grass pinpricked my butt.

Lizzie and I often played together. We shared a room until we were in high school. Lizzie was always smart so I would come home from school and sit her down in the basement with a chalkboard and play school. I would teach her everything I learned that day as well as I could and she always understood it. I would bring home any "extra" copies of worksheets that my teacher had and would have Lizzie do them as her schooling. I would then take her copy and match it up to my corrected worksheet from school. She always got everything right. In fact, she was so bright that she grew up to be valedictorian of her grade school and high school classes.

"Lizzie, let's go walk our babies in their strollers."

We picked up our dolls and went walking in the cul-de-sac that we lived on. Before we knew it, we heard Mom ringing the gold bell she kept by the door to signal that it was dinner time.

Hamburger night. I hated hamburgers. My mother didn't use spices for anything. She was busy enough and spices certainly weren't in the schedule. With ten kids everything was made as plain as possible. That way no one could complain that something was not to their liking. If you wanted to add something to dinner you had to add it yourself because there was a strong likelihood that no one else would want it.

As my sisters and brothers came strolling in from all different places each grabbed a plate from the counter, grabbed some utensils and then took a spot on one of the benches.

Mom would still be standing at the stove and ask, where is so-and-so? If you knew, you replied. If not, you hoped Sean hadn't run away again. Then she would chime into the usual, "Bless us oh Lord, and these our gifts, which we are about to receive through Christ our Lord, Amen."

It was simple daily routines like preparing our dinner plates that made us all very self-sufficient and aware that we had to fend for ourselves.

9

My fourth student arrived within a week. I would need an assistant, so the principal of the school started seeking a teacher's aide. Emma, the youngest of the group, was very frail with very pale skin and bleach blond hair. She would be my only little girl in the class. She could not have been more tiny at 3 years old. Emma barely ate and this was a medical concern because it was contributing to an overall developmental lag. I recognized her refusal to eat as a control issue that I also had as a child. It disturbed me to see a baby as young as Emma with this kind of behavior. She was an extremely angry little girl at such a young age. Screaming was her main form of communication, not words. She would raise the pitch of her voice so high that it was equivalent to scraping a chalkboard. I knew very little about her background. I sensed there was hurt and anger about whatever the situation was. I believed the result of the situation was Emma's acting out, primarily screaming at almost any opportunity as a reaction to the experiences surrounding her.

Her petite mother, who was 6 months pregnant and starting to show, carried Emma into the classroom. My first impression of Emma's mother was of a tired woman (understandably so), who felt helpless to the point of giving up on her situation. She seemed annoyed while having Emma clinging to her. I felt a great deal of compassion for her. She was probably exhausted from holding a child in her belly and on her hip nonstop.

Emma would not get down from her mother's arms despite my assurances. I knew she needed some time to trust the safety of her new surroundings. She rested her head against her mother's chest pouting and hiding from the new environment.

Her mother just smiled and with exaggerated eyes said, "She's not very good at dealing with new situations."

I smiled. "Hello Emma, I'm Miss Maureen." She kept her head nuzzled against her mom and did not respond.

I said, "Emma, I know you love your mommy and are a little scared right now but we are going to have fun at school. Why doesn't Emma come sit on the carpet and join us while we play?"

Despite Emma's mother's pregnant state, she maneuvered herself into a sitting position on the floor with her daughter. I always let my children start off the day with free time. They sat and did whatever they wanted for the first half hour. Then, I would sing my song:

Five more minutes to work and play.
Five more minutes then we'll put our work away.

I announced it was circle time as I guided each child to a spot and Emma and her mother did the same. Phew, Jonas had not tried to sprint out of the classroom. During circle time I did what most teachers did in "normal" classrooms. The children were all sitting and I felt a sense of relief as Emma's mother observed. With the billboard behind me, I said, "Good morning."

"Let's all say, 'Hello Emma.'"

In that second, I decided that "hello" would be our first exercise in communication. So, I went to each child and had them repeat "hello" while looking at Emma as best they could, even if it was just a quick glance in her direction. Emma gave a slight shy smile and nuzzled her head back into her mother.

"Today is Tuesday, the fifth. Andrew, will you put our number on the calendar?"

Andrew had gained so much skill that I knew he could successfully complete this task.

"Thank you Andrew for doing such a good job putting the number on the calendar."

"Jonas, tell me if it is sunny or rainy today?" Jonas typically offered one-word responses so I gave him one-word choices. Jonas didn't respond.

I then asked Jonas to look out the window and tell if it was sunny or rainy today. Jonas loved being asked to look out the window. Jonas loved anything that allowed him to get up and move. He sprinted from the carpet, running to the window and said extremely quickly almost yelling, "Sun-ny."

"Thank you Jonas for telling us it is sunny out."

I walked over, guided him toward the board and said, "We are going to hang up the sunny sign. We are hanging the sunny sign up together." I put my hand over his as we completed the task together and he wiggled away from me. We were both standing once again, so I decided in that moment that the best thing to do was act like we should be standing.

"Miss Maureen is going to sing our Boa-Constrictor song. Everyone can stand up." I began my attempt at singing.

I'm being eaten by a boa constrictor,
I'm being eaten by a boa constrictor,
I'm being eaten by a boa constrictor
and I don't like it very much!
Oh no, oh no, he swallowed my toe!

I would grab my toe or a child's. They would laugh at my simple actions and exaggerations. Andrew had been there the longest so he had the actions down pat. My eyes and affect always helped me a great deal with these children. The size of my eyes helped exaggerate my words, resulting in the children being more attentive to me, sometimes almost staring. They needed extreme examples to get their attention and I was able to give that to them.

By the time I finished my boa constrictor song, Emma was calm and sitting on the floor and not on her mom's lap. Her mom slipped out of the room and we were able to end circle time and go back to free play. This allowed them to find their center and then I would "join" them. Otherwise, the only other real routines we had were snack and there was an entire process to that. We had the washing of hands and sitting in a chair, throwing away trash, brushing teeth after snack and often learning how to line up to go outside after that snack. This would take at least a full hour when in a typical classroom it would take 30 minutes. A great deal of my delays during our routines were from Jonas' sprinting episodes. He was faster than lightning and I didn't have enough hands to grab him so instead I decided to always be very calm about it. This was the approach that I had seen my mother take so many times growing up.

10

I heard my mom yell from downstairs. She had just gotten off the phone.

"Mo & Lizzie, Aunt Josie called to see if you want to go to her play tomorrow night and help out. You would sleepover too."

"Can we?"

"Yes. Just don't give me a problem and ask to stay longer when I tell you it is time to pick you up, OK?"

"We won't."

The next night, Lizzie, my cousin Kristen and I were all running around at the local town theater in the basement. We were in a huge open room full of high school kids getting into their costumes for the opening night of their play.

I was staring with amazement. Everyone seemed so excited and so much older than me. I was envious but also felt important and privileged to go behind the scenes. As I ran up the stairs, I heard my aunt's loud boisterous voice.

"Lady Bugs, where have you been? I need your help. Kristen, I told you I need you at the entrance door and Maureen & Lizzie at the second set of doors on the left. Now, grab those programs and get to work!"

We scrambled hurriedly to our spots handing out the programs. The lights finally dimmed a few times to give the official, 5-minute warning. People hurried out of the restrooms and to their places. The spotlights were in perfect focus as the curtain lifted.

Next, I was off to the lighting booth where I could get a full view of everything. I quietly climbed up the ladder to find my uncle taking control of everything. He is an engineer who created a masterpiece of a set, as professional as any local theater could have. He didn't miss a single detail; it looked fabulous.

I would choose my favorite actor and imagine how I would play the part. I related to acting. After all, I acted everyday as if I were a happy, normal kid. These plays would pull me in emotionally like I had never experienced before. I felt a sense of relief and joy.

I wanted to spend as much time at Aunt Josie's as I could. I was at her house playing UNO with her two youngest daughters the night of the show when she came into the kitchen.

"Maureen, I just spoke to your mom this morning; she wants to pick you and Lizzie up tomorrow morning. She has to run Barbara somewhere so she would like to pick you up then."

I didn't want to leave. I wanted to stay and go to the theater again but I knew better than to complain. I packed my bags in preparation for my mother. In the meantime, we played our hearts out. We cleaned up our UNO game and we all ran out the door and up the ladder to the tree house. It was another world up in that tree house and it was high. We also decided that it was hot! We had a solution for that. We ran back inside, put our bathing suits on, grabbed three black heavy-duty garbage bags from under the sink and headed to the backyard hose. Kristen turned the hose on as Lizzie and I set up the brown bags. Lizzie was first. She got into her bag and sat down and pulled it around her waste. We brought her the hose to fill it up. Wah-la we each had our own personal Jacuzzi. The major difference from the real thing was that the water was absolutely freezing and any bubbles stopped as soon as we were done filling the bag up.

My memories with my cousins were some of the happiest ones from my childhood. We played all day long, nonstop. I didn't have any responsibility other than playing. Aunt Josie gave us our space and took care of us. She never interrupted us, but always stepped away giving us independence while she did her own thing in another room. Still, we were the focus of her day, the "lady bugs." Visits with them were always a nice break from my responsibilities of helping Mom with the younger kids. Life seemed fun and that questioning voice inside me temporarily quieted and calmed.

11

Later that week I learned that I would be having guests in my classroom to observe how we "worked" everyday. My visitors would be Judith and another possible student, with his mom and his speech therapist. They wanted to make sure that my classroom would be the proper place for her little boy.

It was January 5th, 1998. I sat down to write in my journal:

Today went okay. I really do love working with these kids. This is definitely what God put me on this planet to do right now. I'm nervous for tomorrow. This is the FIRST time since my first day of school with Andrew that Judith will be in my classroom solely to observe what I actually do. I don't feel organized and I don't feel like Judith realizes what is really going on in my classroom. I just don't want to be a failure at this. If they sit and observe how unfocused my classroom is my integrity will be questioned and I won't know how to answer because I do not know how to fully explain to these people what I do.

I closed my journal thinking about the fact that my hands were already full, unsure of whether I was really making enough progress with my children. I decided I needed help in my classroom and would ask about the teacher's aide they had told me I would eventually have.

I thought of my next day and what we would do in class. At this point I felt the only exercise book that Judith had given me was becoming boring. We had been doing the color and cut outs for weeks and it just didn't have any allure anymore.

Motor skills were a major challenge for my kids but there were lots of other ways to develop them than through those exercises. So, I decided for the remainder of the year we would alternate activities every few days. I felt it got to the point that the students and I had all grown tired of it.

I often used the outdoors as an extension of the indoor classroom. I remember the first day we saw snow falling from the sky. I immediately said to my class, "Look at the snow falling."

We got their coats on and ran outside for a lesson on snowflakes: how they look and feel, where they come from, anything I could think of while we opened our mouths to the sky and tasted those flakes.

We would often come in from our outside escapades and, like all children, they would need to use the bathroom. I had a single bathroom in my classroom and we used the bathroom in the hall that was used by the rest of the school. It was good for my children to do what their peers did. I had one child in our classroom bathroom, the other children on the carpet playing and another in the "big boy bathroom." Everything seemed fine, as the children played and were a little worn down from just returning from recess. The student in the "big boy bathroom" seemed to be taking a little bit longer than usual so I walked to our classroom doorway to watch for his return. I saw a little boy from the kindergarten walk out of the bathroom and figured he was right behind him. He was definitely right behind him but he seemed to have forgotten something. That something was his clothes.

I started my monologue with a slight smirk.

"You need to go back into the bathroom and put your clothes on. Such and such is naked and needs to put his clothes on. We are at school. We wear clothes at school." He looked up at me as if nothing were unusual and walked back into the bathroom. In the meantime I hoped the other teachers would stay in their classrooms until he was dressed. He did listen and put his clothes back on, but it was certainly at his own pace. These kids were learning by testing their boundaries, just as any child does. Really, my only concern when little challenges happened like that one were how the other teachers and the administration would react. I knew that getting panicky wouldn't help because time did not exist in our classroom; only patience did.

12

My 4th grade teacher, Mrs. Klein, appeared fake in every way. Her makeup and her smile hid her anger and frustration; she also changed her personality when she was around parents. I kept my thoughts to myself because I knew that God didn't want us to dislike people and I didn't want to cause trouble.

Mrs. Klein always wore what I viewed as obnoxiously bright red or pink lipstick. She loved history. I couldn't stand it. History was worse than English because it required even more memorization. I never understood the questions at the end of each history section. They made me want to scream. They would ask a question but the answer was usually worded very differently from the question. I could only find the answer when it restated the question. I couldn't understand what I was reading; there was too much information. I would look at the pictures and often start to "zone out" or look at the shapes that the words formed as paragraphs. My mother didn't understand why I didn't get it. She would try to explain why history was so interesting but it didn't help. I usually got her to answer my homework questions for me. To her it was fun; to me it was hell. Probably equivalent to the hell that my oldest brother, Sean (who was 15 years old at the time) caused her.

As I grew up, I grew more scared of Sean. His naturally curly, out-of-control brown hair was a metaphor for his consistently out-of-control behavior. He was small for his age but trim and athletic. I have a few memories of Sean in grade school, most of which consisted of him running away from home. He would be gone for hours and would usually show up once darkness hit. He was the most outwardly rebellious child in my family. I hated his fits and tantrums. He yelled and cursed for what seemed like any reason he could think of.

His high school years are most vivid in my memory. He would come home and make huge plates of food and watch MTV in the dark. He would tell anyone who entered his space to leave him alone. Most of the time, "his space" was our family room. But, I was allowed in there. It wasn't just his space. I thought that if I sat nearby without saying anything he might feel a tiny bit better.

At 6 years old, I didn't understand why he was drawn to the family room so much. I concluded that he must have just liked the TV. The environment of that room was what stood out most to me. The floor was covered in a brownish-orange shaggy wall-to-wall carpet that made the room feel dark and sad to me. It was dark because it only had half windows. It was part basement, part above ground. The fireplace was a nice touch, but we really didn't use it that much. If I were an adult at the time I would have changed the rug at least. I was always very aware of my surroundings, noticing color, textures, and placement of furniture. I liked things to be neat and clean, with everything in its place. I needed to create some type of order outside to balance the chaos that I felt.

"Maureen, do you have homework today?"

"Yes."

"Well then you better stop hanging out with your brother, honey, and go do it."

"Okay, Mom."

What is she talking about? I wasn't hanging out with him. I just didn't feel like doing anything but resting somewhere. When I "watched" TV I never really watched it. It was my down time to zone out. Most of the time, I had no idea what they were saying or doing on TV. I didn't listen to the TV. I only listened to the conversation going on in my head and observed my surroundings or the pictures on the screen, the clothes people wore and the rooms they were in. It appeared as if the TV "pulled" me in, but in fact my own thoughts had nothing to do with what was on the screen.

I didn't mind doing my spelling homework: I just had to copy a word five times on those large double lines. I was good at penmanship; it was like drawing a picture or connect-the-dots. I never memorized those words when I wrote them 5 times in a row. I was only interested in the shapes the letters formed. I tended to see things differently and often, literally. So, when it came to writing letters, I didn't concentrate on why I was writing the words, whether it be for spelling or vocabulary. Instead, I focused on what interested me, which was the visual result. Therefore, I looked at writing as another art class and what I focused on most was making all the letters look perfect, like art. I understood the concept that many letters formed words but I often found myself lost when trying to pronounce them. For some reason, I couldn't make sense of how to put together certain words when there were so many sounds to pronounce. At some point, it became too much to put together and it didn't interest me to try because I had other things on my mind.

Even though my mom didn't know what was going on in my head, it was apparent that I was unhappy. She wanted some type of an explanation for my unhappiness so she brought me to a woman who tested my brain. She mostly asked me to do things I felt I was good at, primarily puzzles. I was great at puzzles and felt like this lady understood me. She was patient and I trusted her kindness. I didn't mind going back to see her. My mother, on the other hand, was extremely emotional and clingy. I distinctly remember watching her speak with the doctor. I felt badly for my mother because I think I was scaring her. She didn't know how to help me. I was like another Sean but didn't complain. My mom always tried so hard to smile and act like everything was fine even when I knew it wasn't. She always referred to God during these times too. By mid-year in the fourth grade I was struggling with history and math was almost as difficult for me. I withdrew. That was the first year I remember being anorexic. For some reason, I became very conscious of my body and how I wanted it to look. I felt imperfect and I wouldn't let an ounce of fat on my body to add to the feeling of imperfection.

As an adult, I finally read the psychological analysis the "nice lady" wrote about me.

"Maureen is here for testing because her parents are concerned that she has withdrawn socially in school as well as at home with her siblings."

She was on the nose with that one. More than anything, I was worried that my mom was spending money on me. I knew how hard it was for her to pay and she had a lot on her plate, more than I could ever imagine.

My mother told me the nice lady determined that I had "perceptual problems." For instance, if you asked me to look at 3 circles and determine which lids fit on top of which bottom I would mix them up. Apparently, even though I scored in the superior range on my performance IQ (object assembly, block design, etc), discrepancies in my abilities caused my verbal and visual perception to be a little askew. Did this also mean that my perception of the world around me was askew? My mother used to say that it was. She would say, "Maureen, I think your learning disability gives you a slightly wrong picture of things." For a long time I believed my mother and as a result, constantly questioned my own judgment. She would say this if I would mention things like thinking I looked a little heavy in a picture. I was always surprised to hear that I looked thin in a picture. People's perception of me often surprised me. It was another reminder that I interpreted things differently than those around me.

Consequently, I remained a quiet observer, taking things in, rather than speaking my own mind (which I didn't have much confidence in). I now know that what I thought of as misunderstandings around me were actually understandings on my part. I also learned that my classification as learning disabled was the result of scoring in the superior range of visual perception. Learning disabilities are calculated by comparison of the scores in each of the areas tested. Because I scored superior in one area and average in another (but not below average) I was classified as disabled. Therefore, if I had scored average in my visual perception I would not have been classified because both areas would have been equal and consistent. So, ironically, what could be considered a strength was classified as a weakness, and this made me feel that I was lacking in some way.

13

Our visitor from the previous week, Michael, would become my fifth student. He was the most severely impaired of all the children. He had been classified as autistic and/or PDD. He was speechless and made virtually no attempts at communication with the outside world. At six years old, he was the oldest of all the children. I had learned through research that children basically form their personalities by age 5. Because of this, the element of time was crucial in getting through to Michael before he would habituate an internalized dialogue.

I had seen his mother pull up to the building; the first glimpse I saw of Michael was 20 minutes later. This is how long it took his mother, Jane, to coax him into the school. Michael had made it to the hallway and his mother was clearly frustrated and trying not to be annoyed. You could see the exhaustion on her face. She was a beautiful woman about 5'8" tall with blond hair. Her son had inherited her good looks. She was well-educated and you could clearly see that she wanted an explanation for the circumstance she was in. No parent expects that their child will be non-communicative. The look of despair in her face made this very clear. I tried to be as positive as possible.

"Hello," I said with a huge smile to the brown-haired, handsome and well-dressed young boy who was almost as tall as me.

His mother walked ahead of him. "Hi, we are just having a problem getting Michael to come into school. He's just a little tired today."

"No problem. Let me see if I can assure Michael that this is going to be fun."

I walked down the hall to the door of the school and met him there.

"Hello Michael," I said calmly.

He was turned toward the wall and did not give any sign of acknowledgment.

"I'm Miss Maureen. It's so nice to see you. I would love for you to come into the classroom. I have to go back to the classroom so your mom is going to help you come into the classroom." I stepped away and went back to my classroom door.

Jane walked back over to Michael. He turned to his mother and walked a few steps toward the classroom. This went on for another 10 minutes until his mother coerced him through the classroom door.

Michael rocked back and forth from foot to foot as he stood with his legs a little more than shoulder-width apart in the middle of the classroom carpet. He stared up at the alphabet border that was placed high above the chalkboard. He would occasionally hum while rocking.

I said, "That's great, Jane, thanks for your help." I imagine Jane was relieved, but at the same time felt some hesitation as she left.

I sat on the carpet with the rest of my class as I attempted to have circle time with my students. "Circle" was not a concept my students understood; "circle time" was more like let's-just-sit-anywhere-on-the-carpet time. The real point was to get everyone sitting within a reasonable radius of one another to create a shared experience.

Michael remained standing, rocking and staring at the alphabet the entire time. I let him do whatever he wanted. I was giving him the freedom to explore our class on his terms. I let him observe the first day so that he could "take in" his new surroundings.

After we left the carpet and began our classroom tasks, Michael took a book from the shelf and sat in a beanbag chair. He was comfortable; my objective for the day, to make sure he felt comfort without pressure, had been met. I didn't know this would be my objective. It just naturally developed as I observed. I could sense he had enough stress just trying to get into the classroom. He was such a sweet boy. He read his book over and over again, for at least an hour while I played with the rest of the class.

At one point, I sat down next to Michael just so he could feel what it would be like to be near me. He needed to trust my presence.

I sat with him and began my usual monologue, hoping for dialogue. After about two minutes, Michael stood up from his beanbag and walked in a circle. This was his way of showing that he was finished with the interaction. Michael often walked in "circles" or different directions. His body language conveyed his emotional confusion.

Michael was the most solitary of the children. He would be my biggest challenge. He seemed to be deep into his own world and yet he was clearly the most intellectual. He was the only child who was able to read and was fascinated by books and numbers. I often had to lure him back into the group. His heart was big and his needs were, too. I saw Judith one day as she was passing by with her usual smile.

"Hi Judith."

"Hi Maureen. I can see the children are all doing so well."

"Thanks Judith, but I really need an aide. There are just too many kids for me to handle."

"I know. I'll talk with the office and see what the delay is and what we can do."

"Thank you."

I understood Michael's sensitivity to his surroundings and I also felt that in order to get through to him I needed an extra hand to juggle things.

14

We finished up our day. I headed out the door to change for track practice. My dad ran the track team on the weekends. It was one of the only ways we got to see him. He wrote the workouts and gave them to my mother who dutifully ran the practices for us during the school week. I changed, ran out to the car, went to the field, did my running, got home and did the usual routine of homework, TV and then Mom called for dinner.

Dad was rarely at home for dinner but for some reason he made it that night. I remember my mom and dad talking as they walked toward the kitchen table. Our kitchen table was a dark mahogany rectangle shape with benches along the sides in order to maximize seating space. My father sat at the head of the table as my mother walked food over to the table and said grace out loud.

"Bless us, oh Lord and these our gifts, which we are about to receive from Your Bounty through Christ our Lord, Amen. We also need to say a prayer for my cousin Phyllis and her two sons who live in California. Their dad, David, died today. Amen."

Something within uncharacteristically compelled me to ask more. "What happened to their father, Mom?"

"He was killed."

"How?"

"He was an actor and was filming a movie in a trailer park. He went running after a man who robbed a poor elderly couple that lived there…and the man turned around and killed him."

"How old are the boys?" I asked.

"Their oldest is the same age as you."

I didn't say anything. I was upset. Thoughts of the boys whose father was killed kept running through my mind. I prayed to David that night. I prayed to David and for that family for months because it was the most horrible thing that I had ever heard.

I went into school the next day asking my teacher to add my distant cousins to our intention list. I was disturbed for weeks by this tragedy. I constantly thought of how those boys felt and prayed to God to please help them.

I continued those internal thoughts one fall Saturday afternoon as I ran back and forth, unaware of where I was supposed to be on the field at my soccer game. I had a tough time with soccer. I liked dribbling the ball but I just could not get the concept of being off sides or staying at your position. I was not a fighter in team sports; I didn't have the aggressive desire to win. So, I knew I was an average player and the fact that I was a cross-country runner was a major factor in my value to the team. Each game I played, I made sure to stay in the general area that I was told to and hoped that I didn't get called for being off sides. I didn't have time for what I thought were silly games with so many thoughts going on in my head. I would hang back and just follow the general direction that everyone was playing in.

That Saturday was a particularly busy one. Our annual town fair was being held. The vendors had tables: there was food, face painting, and even hayrides.

I was lost in my own thoughts as usual on the soccer field. Then I heard a siren. Our 5th grade teacher, Mrs. Gray, told us to stop and say a prayer anytime we heard a siren. So, that's exactly what I did. I saw the minuteman truck speed past the field and to the other fields diagonally across the road. My body and mind froze as an intense feeling went through me. I became very worried and nervous for whomever that ambulance was for so I stopped right in the middle of the game and said a prayer for the person. After my game I found out that the ambulance was for my younger 4-year-old brother. He had been on the hayride and the driver had gone too close to the iron fence and sliced off his finger. My older cousin, Margaret, happened to be on the ride with Timothy and was the one who first realized that Timothy's finger was cut. She yelled to the driver who was only a few years older than herself, "STOP, STOP!" She pulled Timothy off the tractor, grabbed his finger and wrapped it in what was her forest green sweatshirt now forever stained with red blood. She ran right through the middle of another soccer game squeezing Timothy's finger into her shirt. She reached my parents and the next thing that was heard was the sound of the ambulance that literally stopped me in my tracks on that field.

I noted my gut instinct and how clear it felt that something wasn't right. I imagine it's the same instinct a mother has when she knows something is wrong with her child.

15

Shortly after Michael had arrived, I was happy to hear that the search for my new aide was done. She would be starting the following week. I was a little insulted by the authoritarian way that this was done. I was the teacher and the administration didn't even have me meet the person that would be working with me 8 hours a day. It felt disrespectful and made it apparent to me they did not fully comprehend the scope of what was going on in my classroom. To the principal and vice principal, my class was unexplainable. They could not see any order because I did not run my classroom like the rest of the school was run and my children were frequently outdoors. I sensed they felt the disorder was a result of not using "chips," the reinforcement tactic that was the basis for the entire school curriculum. Each child was given a chip throughout the day once they completed a task or did what the teacher asked. They could then use these chips for a treat. I knew these children did not need chips in order to be motivated to embrace life. These children were operating on a different frequency, and just as I was insulted by my superiors who misunderstood me, they would be insulted by what would be to them meaningless tactics.

That next Monday morning my aide was introduced to me. This young woman, who was just barely the legal age to be working a full-time job, immediately struck me as the wrong person to be my aide. I tried not to be frustrated by my circumstances.

The next time I saw Judith I said, "Judith, she is trying her best but she's not what we need." I looked at her and Judith nodded and walked on.

I was exhausted and giving every ounce of what I could, but this was not going to help. I believed the principal was a kind lady, but her understanding was very old-fashioned, overly cautious, and her approach to solving problems was very rote. The fact that she created this circumstance, even though she assured me it was temporary, created an additional layer of stress and frustration for me, and I feared being distracted by this and unable to be present for the kids. I had no choice but to deal with the situation and make it work as best I could. I did what I had been doing since day one: I took a deep breath and said, I will figure it out, there's a reason for everything. I managed my new assistant much like I did my children, with love and respect. She did not have an aggressive bone in her body and to me this was a good thing. I didn't have to worry about her losing her temper. The next time I saw Judith I inquired about a replacement.

Judith assured me that she would speak with the principal. I worried that the administration would continue to address this problem without communicating with me directly. But God took care of me: I was able to meet Suri when she came in to be interviewed.

Suri was a blessing. She was positive and a couple of years older than me. She was married and lived an Orthodox Jewish life. The combination of the two gave her a very grounding energy. We were a team. We divided our responsibilities up by our strengths. She had a certain connection with Jonas. A big part of that connection was their shared religious beliefs in Orthodox Judaism. As a result Suri understood his daily life. Since Jonas and Michael were our biggest challenges and therefore, the most in need of individual attention, Suri became the main mentor for Jonas, and I became Michael's. I loved having someone to work with who was so committed to her beliefs and values. I respected her a great deal for her dedication to a religion that a large part of society finds extreme and outdated. She would teach me about her way of life and beliefs. There is a pureness to the Orthodox Jewish religion that is refreshing. I could only parallel it to what I knew and learned all those years in Catholic school.

I did not know until months after working with her that she wore a wig every day because it was customary in Orthodox Judaism for a woman to cover her natural hair in public and only allow the husband to see this part of her. I also learned that men and women had separate bathing areas when they went to swim. The fact that they swam separately was fascinating to me. Suri said her prayers before she ate and this meant a great deal to me. I had been taught before dinner to say grace but I never continued this ritual. She brought that back into my life. She reminded me of the fact that praying before anything you eat raises the vibration of the food that you are experiencing and are putting into your body. God had sent me another one of his angels. Suri reminded me to not lose the faith that I was taught as a child and it was working.

    She would say things like, "When my husband met you he said you were a born teacher because he could tell by your voice. You have the voice of a teacher." I smiled, thanking God for Suri and the patience that she restored to my life. She was another reminder to me that God was there just as he had been so many times before. I simply had to open my eyes to see it.

16

As expected in my family, I was still running track, and I remember my desire to be as thin as possible being a big part of my internal dialogue. It was like a "fill in," helping me avoid any down time that I might have and distracting me from the chaos in the world around me. Instead, I redirected the chaos inward; when I felt angry or overwhelmed, I would deny myself food in order to gain some sense of balance and control. I knew I had track every afternoon and the one major reason I looked forward to it was it forced me to run off any unwanted calories I may have consumed that day.

There were few things I still looked forward to during the school day, and they all involved leaving the classroom. I loved to have art, music, or even history at this point, just because they were taught by different teachers and they offered a change in routine. Our seventh grade teacher, Mrs. Cohen, had taught us English in sixth grade as well. She was not someone who read straight out of a book. She was a woman who just rambled off rules to you about the English grammar and expected you to abide by them and commit them to memory within seconds of hearing them.

This was a nightmare for me as it was in stark contrast to the way I learned best. The one positive thing about her was that she always did class exercises by the order in which we sat. At this point, I developed my own little strategies to deal with any challenges I had in different subjects. The fact that she did everything in the order of the workbook exercises allowed me to always count up in advance (while the other questions were being answered) and find which question was going to be mine. I would figure out the answer before she got to me and make it appear as if I were normal and had no delays in my ability to figure out the answer to a question. This was just one coping mechanism I could put into practice with her so that I could do things at my own pace. However, she had an unpredictable mean streak to her and, as a result, 7th grade was a dark year for me. Mrs. Cohen had a stubby look that matched the roughness of the rest of her. I didn't like her energy. She knew I didn't like her and that probably fueled her dislike for me. She expected me to measure up to my older siblings who were all straight A students. To her, I was the dunce.

The ironic thing was that she was a mother of 8 children so I thought she would be kinder and more understanding of children and their different strengths and weaknesses. Instead, she was an angry, frustrated woman and her skin and voice reflected this. She had the skin of a smoker, dried out and tanned. She had the voice of one, too, scratchy and frog-like. As I observed her more each day and listened to her very light comments referring to her own life I had a very good hunch that her home environment was a bit dysfunctional. She probably compensated for her lack of control of her own children by dominating our classroom. I resented her for this. I just found it interesting that someone who probably didn't want to deal with her own children was compelled to be the teacher of a classroom of children she felt she could control.

Because of my resentment and dread of having to deal with her, mornings were the worst. I would frequently plot to leave the classroom and never come back. I didn't know how to get off the grounds without anyone seeing me because the school was practically wall-to-wall windows. I thought of suicide. I would imagine the world without Maureen Marshall in it. Would it matter? I didn't feel like I belonged. Who would find me? How would they react? Who would care and who would it hurt most? I decided it would hurt my parents and siblings most of all. I couldn't do that to them, and knew I had to stay on this earth. I didn't know what to do. I asked my mother for a mental day off almost weekly. I would refuse to go to school when denied. She knew I was near the edge, just not how close. I would never tell my mother about my suicidal thoughts or about wanting to run away. She had enough to worry about with Sean's running away episodes and his consistently rebellious behavior. My mother was emotionally maxed out. I wondered why God surrounded me with so many adults who made me feel as if I needed to help them more than myself.

On a Wednesday afternoon, Mrs. Cohen decided that we had to squeeze in one more subject before lunch. She belted out her usual commanding orders.

"Take out your English workbook homework from last night."

Unenthusiastically, I bent over to pull out my book, listening to the usual chatter around me.

"Maureen, stop talking. Just take out your book," I heard Mrs. Cohen say.

I was dreaming of my half peanut butter and jelly sandwich, cup of milk and Hostess chocolate cupcake.

I looked directly at her and uncharacteristically replied.

"I was not talking."

"Yes you were. Now stop it."

I looked at her again and insisted, "I was not talking."

She looked at me again, "Yes you were."

"You know what?" I said, "You are an asshole. I just told you I wasn't talking. If I were talking, I wouldn't insist that I wasn't. I don't know what your problem is and why you feel the need to nitpick me. The only reason I can think of is that you're an asshole." Then I walked out of the room, slamming the door behind me.

My mom kept me home for a whole week after that episode. I simply couldn't keep my anger inside any more and she knew it. I was anorexic (about 70 lbs.) and refused to eat breakfast and no more than my half a sandwich for lunch, saying I wasn't hungry and claiming not to like anything else. I got mad if my mom asked if she could make me a whole sandwich. My eating habits were barely discussed; I imagine my mom was afraid to say anything. Besides, I didn't like to eat a lot because I constantly had stomachaches from the stress of the school day. I never once complained about that to my mom. I knew what my stomachaches were from and she couldn't help that. I had to keep on telling myself what a lucky kid I was. I was healthy and had a mother and father. It didn't matter that there was nothing I enjoyed or felt good at. This was life. I would make the best of my situation but literally felt as if I was dragging my body everywhere I went. I knew I couldn't share such crazy, dark thoughts with anyone so they stayed within me.

I talked to my classmates only when spoken to. I wouldn't dare be unkind to anyone who hated school even half as much as I did. That year, I went to a "tutor" who made me feel somewhat competent and somehow helped me get through. She never got mad at me, even when I didn't do my assignments. I appreciated her understanding.

My final year of grade school was less work. I did what I was supposed to and didn't have any major outbursts. I was left alone and not bothered by our eighth grade teacher, Mrs. Krane.

Months before graduation, we finalized our yearbook. We had handed in our personal pages with our quotes beneath our names. I would look back at the quote I chose and almost marvel at where my brain was at that point in my life. I chose, "I like to make people laugh, so they see things seriously," by Stephen Wright.

Mrs. Krane stood in front of the class and announced we would do the final additions. We were doing a yearbook vote on everyone's dominant characteristic. Each student had to leave the room for a few minutes so that everyone could discuss the person's trait.

"Let's start with John. John, please go for a walk down the hallway and I'll send someone out to get you when we are finished."

Shain goes out to retrieve John and brings him back to the classroom.

"John you were voted Most Likely to Succeed."

"Mo, would you be so kind as to take a walk?"

"Sure," I replied (with a quiet smile as I looked down at the ground).

Erin brings me back into the classroom.

I didn't know what to expect, I just didn't want to get anything about being motherly or something I felt was predictable.

"Maureen, we have voted you Most Popular."

I thought everyone looked at me as dorky, slow, weird and (most of all) not bright. Why were my internal perceptions of myself so drastically different from those of others?

17

The sixth child to join our class was Brad. Brad had Attention Deficit Hyperactivity Disorder. He was fully verbal but had auditory processing difficulties and his words were frequently delayed. He could not control his body or his words. As a result, he was frequently getting in fights and grabbing things out of other children's hands. He was a chunky, very strong little boy who didn't know his own strength.

His mother was scared of him. She didn't understand how to control him and set no limits. She wanted to be nice all the time and her niceness was leading to major discipline problems with her child. He did not know what was socially acceptable behavior and this was costing him big time. Discipline in an undisciplined environment was my goal with Brad. I felt this was the easiest of all my feats. He had not shut out the outside world; he was alert and aware. His awareness needed to be carefully guided so that he could begin to understand the emotions that consequently triggered his physical impulsivity. This I could do often with a few words. He tested me and quickly learned what was acceptable behavior. I knew from my gut when he truly did something unintentionally, and I would explain firmly the correct behavior and find specific ways to enforce my words. "Time out" is what so many people call it nowadays, but we didn't call it that. We called it "sit down and gather your thoughts and feelings." This was practical and didn't have such a punitive connotation to it. A ritual that also encouraged slowing down was naptime.

I recall naptime being my favorite activity in kindergarten. Yes, naptime. I loved the silence and the fact that we were forced to stop everything. I remember the peace I felt stretched out on my little piece of cut carpet. I didn't want it to be over, but I knew most of my classmates did. I wondered if any of my students felt the same sense of relief at naptime that I had felt as a child.

Naptime was another skill they could bring home with them. So, with my kindergarten years in mind, Suri and I said, "We're exhausted and the children are exhausted. Naptime sounds perfect."

The concept was perfect, but actually creating the reality was far from it. Sleeping was a major issue with many of our children. Jonas could not sit still and at home he would only go to bed when utterly exhausted. Michael would sleep but it was a concern how he slept. You could put him to bed and he would not leave that room for anything until his mother came in to get him the next morning.

About two months into Michael being in my class his mother approached me one day and said, "We are seeing some amazing changes in his behavior at home. When I put him to bed last night, I also went to bed and all of a sudden we heard something outside our bedroom door. It was Michael. He was sitting on the stairs outside our door. He has never done this before. He has never left his room after being put to bed." He wanted to communicate and he was no longer letting that bedroom door stop him. He wanted to let his mommy and daddy into his world. I think I was just as amazed as his mother. Something was working.

So many parents take such a simple act as the knocking on their door from a child for granted. This was a miracle to these parents. This was the behavior of a "normal" child. I saw the pain being released and peace entering that mother's life.

The children who gave us the most difficulty during naptime were our over-stimulated Jonas and Brad. For the most part, Suri took Jonas as her responsibility during naptime and I took the rest unless she was overtired and then we would switch. Suri would very gently lean her weight onto Jonas, giving him pressure on his arms and legs to calm him. He was learning how to rest but it was not an easy lesson.

Emma didn't have a problem lying down because she was only three years old and frail from her malnourishment. She really needed naptime a great deal. Brad, for the most part, rested if we gave him some sort of stimulant for his hands: either a Beanie Baby or something that he could squeeze. Andrew was so normalized at this point that he did exactly what we asked of him. Simon was a piece of cake.

Despite my exhaustion, as per the request of Michael's mother and speech therapist, I tried to write in his journal each day. I was to record the goals and accomplishments he made. This was difficult for me because I was not exactly approaching it as a speech therapist would. I was performing speech therapy but in a slightly different way. Things were not structured as a therapy session was. I was dealing more with emotional struggles than with ones concerning language.

The therapist and Michael's mother were more than happy with the progress he was making. He had made more progress in my classroom than he had anywhere else (and he had seen the most reputable doctors in the field). However, they often felt I was not working up to Michael's potential. The fact of the matter was, I knew Michael's abilities and especially understood his intelligence. To me, however, this had nothing really to do with what I was trying to accomplish. He could develop intellect on his own. It was pulling him out of himself that was his biggest challenge. I would say yes very respectfully to his mother and his therapist's suggestions just as they very respectfully gave opinions of concepts that I should be working on. They would stress how he understood very complex sequencing and I should add more advanced words or concepts to his goals. I wanted to say no, I'm sorry, that's just not what I am dealing with here. That is not the root of Michael's issues. But I couldn't.

His therapist was always kind in her words and often complimented me on what she called my natural intuition, but I believe she felt a need to guide me. She was knowledgeable, knew all the lexicon of the field, all the terminologies that make one sound very educated but she didn't fully speak my language. I was new to the field so my speech pathology lexicon was limited. I would turn to Judith when I felt pressured by this insecurity.

I'd say, "Judith, can you help me out because I don't know what I should say or write so that they feel like I am on their level." She was very kind and would gladly say, "Just do this."

About every two weeks I would hand Michael's marble-colored notebook to his mom to give to his therapist. Much to my surprise, when I first received her comments back I couldn't help but notice any grammatical errors I had made would be corrected with her pen as well as a kind note at the end with suggestions in regards to goal setting for Michael. Those corrections could have been from his mother when looking over the notes. However, the handwriting coincided with the written notes so I concluded it was the therapist making corrections.

The one thing that I did learn from the principal of this school was that you should say 2 to 3 positives when talking about a child to a parent and, only after those positives, say the negative. This was what I felt his therapist was essentially doing to me when she would compliment my accomplishments and then make corrections in my notebook. I found it interesting that someone would feel compelled to fix grammatical errors that were only being shared between two individuals without ever verbally mentioning something about those corrections. Despite the grammatical errors that flashed back in red at me, much like the errors of my school years, I knew I was the one getting through to Michael and that was what mattered most.

I also knew the underlying issue was that I wasn't fully conscious of what was making me so successful at what I was doing so I had no grounding to explain my viewpoint. I wasn't a know-it-all but his progress spoke for itself and they said less and less as the year went on. To appease them I created the façade that more complex concepts were a priority in making Michael better. I wasn't going to let my ego or emotional issues take away from Michael's progress so I bit my lip and continued to work hard and pray for inspiration.

18

High school was stressful but an improvement from grade school. My Catholic school education was continued at The Academy, an all-girls private high school three towns away and run by the Sisters of Charity. The marble-faced structures were set back on acres of land that contained classrooms within. They rose high into the sky and were more beautiful to the eye than I could have imagined.

As relieved as I was to be out of grade school, I still hated mornings and looked forward to almost nothing. I just felt like I was on a train ride that continued to repeat itself and wouldn't let me off. There was something more to life that I was missing but I didn't know where or how to find it. My homework took me hours to do every night. I would typically stay up until at least 1:30 A.M. doing it.

I would pull myself out of bed every morning and get into the shower in a trance, dizzy from exhaustion. Sometimes I would hit my head on the shower wall because I was so disoriented that I would lose my balance. Starving myself didn't help either. I still refused to eat breakfast. I never felt pretty enough and never could be too thin. I didn't count calories but refused to eat what I thought was "too much" food. I didn't have a scale but made up my own way of determining if I was too fat. Each morning in the shower I would line the profile of my stomach up to the width of the shower tile squares. If for some reason my stomach went a little beyond that one square I knew not to eat too much that day.

Fortunately, high school didn't have carpools. Freshman year I would wait at the bus stop with my long hair soaking wet. I didn't have time to dry my hair as I always got up so late, and it was an uncomfortable, hellish experience. I would stand at the bus stop on cold days starving with hair that would literally freeze in separate locks. It didn't help that I had my plaid skirt rolled up as much as it could be, giving me the least coverage possible. This was what the Catholic girls did to rebel; we hiked up our skirts and pushed down our socks.

Theresa stood at the bus stop with me. She was very tall with pin-straight brownish-blond hair that fell down her back, long legs, and long features. She didn't look you in the eye when she spoke and was slow to respond at times, but she was bright.

I said, "Hi Theresa."

She responded with a smile, "Hi Maureen."

She continued, "I was up late finishing up the cover for my report for Sr. Jerry."

"Oh, I know, I didn't go to bed until 2 A.M."

She responded with shock, "2 A.M.? I went to bed at 10:30 and I'm tired, I don't know how you stay up that late. My parents wouldn't let me."

My response was, "Yeah, my parents don't say anything, they just go to bed."

Then she would zone out, staring for about 3 or 4 minutes and start up a new conversation. She was socially different because of her lack of eye contact and extra long pauses. I understood Theresa's zoning out stare. I didn't care what "label" she fit into. She was kind, so we were friends.

By sophomore year, Amy, a classmate from grade school who continued high school with me, got her license and would pick me up every morning. You could hear the screech of the brakes, as she would round the corner in her mom's old station wagon and honk her horn (an unbearable sound at 7 A.M. in the morning). I would run out with my soaking wet hair and a bulging fifty-pound L.L. Bean backpack of books and somehow make it to the brown-paneled door. Reliably, I would find her brushing her long brown hair. Amy was overweight but it really didn't matter because she was absolutely beautiful. Her skin was flawless and when you looked at her face the contrast of her dark brown hair and piercing green eyes was stunning. I always told her that.

The car ride was always a gut-wrenching experience. The tape player would be blasting music out of the poor quality speakers. With the desire to make it sound better she was constantly switching the songs. Meanwhile, the cigarette dangling from her mouth always needed to be ashed. She was a horrendous driver, concentrating on everything but driving. I was constantly telling her to look out for cars and she was always jamming on the brakes. In all that we only got into one fender bender – which was amazing, given the odds I was facing each day.

When we finally made it to The Academy, it took more than ten minutes to first cross the railroad tracks in front of the school and then the front lawn to actually reach those distinguished and timeworn buildings. I was consistently late to homeroom. I would blame it on the fact that I was one of ten children; there was too much going on in the morning to get me there on time. In a family my size, someone was always missing their usual means of transportation to one of the many different private schools we went to that were in all different directions. It could be the bus, the train or a car ride that was missed and this resulted in one of my parents scrambling to figure out how we would get there and ultimately someone else being late. Someone could have a special extra-curricular activity going on, or a sports event. Someone might get sick. The baby might have thrown up. The occurrences were countless and we knew no other way of life. The majority of my teachers found the size of my family alone incomprehensible and usually let it slide.

I kept the same routines I had in grade school. After school I would go to a sport, whether it be soccer, track or lacrosse. From there I would go home, eat a bowl of cereal (I was always famished by then) and head upstairs to tackle my grueling homework. As I sat at my desk (which was situated in front of a window) I would often drift into a daze that would ultimately be interrupted by my mother calling from downstairs, "Dinner, let's go!" I would walk down to the kitchen to find the smell of spaghetti sauce again. I was sick of eating pasta. On a good night we would have meatballs with the sauce but not very often. We had three kids in college at the time and dinners were not always on the affordable list. I remember days coming home from school starving, and finding that cereal and milk were all we had in the cabinets. No one outside of our family knew this. How could we not have enough money for food when we went to the most prestigious and expensive private schools available to us? This was a deep dark secret that we knew not to discuss.

 I had three close friends in high school but didn't even tell them the half of it. I knew it would just embarrass my parents so I was silent about our struggles. Kelsie, Blaire, and Amy, each in their own way, helped me survive high school. I didn't like the so-called popular girls because I thought they were idiots. Their focus in life was the guys and whether or not they hooked up with them. They liked to appear older than they were and I found that annoying. So, I minded my own business, being pleasant and remaining true to who I wanted to be.

 I sometimes felt like a bad person because I dismissed a lot of people as silly or considered them a waste of my time. I would rather not have a conversation talking about others. My constant disappointment in people led me to question myself. I prayed to God one night before going to bed, desperately asking him to give me a clear sign of whether I was good or bad. Despite my good girlfriends, I still felt a void. No matter what I explained to them, they didn't understand the constant responsibilities that I felt being one of ten. Most of all, I felt the financial burden that I created for parents that worked very hard. My parents thought they were successfully repressing the stress they felt, but it permeated our lives and made me feel guilty and alienated. The burden made me feel miserable and I didn't know how to fix it.

 I was waiting for a sign the next day. I went to a high school ice hockey game that night to watch the all-boys private school play. The "thing to do" was to stand outside the rink afterwards and talk to the athletes. I would talk to whomever I knew and go home.

 Alison, a classmate, sat next to me on the bus the following day. She was popular among the athletes primarily because of what I believed to be promiscuous behaviors.

"Hi Ali, what's up?"

"Well actually, you know Terrance on the hockey team, right?"

"Yeah, of course I do. He's the only sophomore who's good enough to play Varsity. He's hot too."

"Well, he saw you last night when you were standing near me and asked me if I knew you and other questions about you. He asked if I would give him your number so that he could give you a call. He thinks you're really cute."

I was in shock. He was a popular, handsome guy who could call anyone he wanted. Of course I played it cool.

"Yeah, sure, go ahead."

"Great, I'll give it to him tonight, I'm sure he will call you later this week."

All I could think of was my prayer to God. Terrance obviously saw something good in me and God was speaking to me through Terrance.

Two nights later, Tucker (who went to the same high school as Terrance) walked into the house after another hockey game. He was in a state of shock.

"Tucker, what's wrong?"

"You know Kevin's brother, Terrance, the one who plays on the Varsity team?"

"Of course I know who he is."

"He died tonight."

"What?"

"He died. He was on the ice and all of a sudden he was doubled over in pain. They think his appendix burst."

I couldn't believe it. Was this a bizarre coincidence or a lesson about life?

It was that summer that my mother announced that we would be going to her cousin Phyllis's in August for an extended family reunion that we had about every 5 years. Both of my grandparents came from families of 8 and our reunions were filled with a minimum of 200 people. Only a handful of those people I actually knew. I was curious to hear that Phyllis's family had moved back East a few years prior and that I would finally meet the sons I had prayed for. I went with the agenda of befriending her son, Connor.

    I sat on the vinyl blue bench in the back of our Astro van in silence while the usual nonsense went on in our over-packed car. All ten of us were packed in like sardines as I blocked everyone out and observed the windy roads and the suburbs that we drove through. They were all very old, large homes that were manicured to perfection. We pulled off to a very private side street and made our way back to a beautiful brick home built into a hill. We piled out of the car; the house was as elegant as the homes I had been noticing on our way there. Everything looked perfect to me, which was rare. The entranceway had hardwood floors and ornate rugs and warmly-adorned walls. We walked straight to the back of the house where there was a family room with a casual dining area. I saw a Norman Rockwell painting, which I later discovered was authentic. I was always amazed by paintings. We didn't have paintings in our home, but had large family portraits instead. I was curious so I walked around the house not touching a thing but looking at everything as if it was a museum. Sconces were placed throughout the house; it was like heaven.

    I finally met Connor and followed him up to the fourth floor attic, which was covered in red carpet and had a pair of bunk beds built into the natural architecture of the attic room. I loved this room. Connor sat with me on the floor of that room along with some other of our cousins. He seemed like a tough guy. I expected to meet someone softer. He talked up things but I knew this was a front to cover up what was really going on inside him. He sat with me on the floor that day and he noticed that my necklace was coming loose. As he fixed it I felt calmed by his fumbling fingers. He was kind. I didn't want to leave that feeling or that room but we had to go back downstairs and be with the rest of the company.

    As we drove away that day, an intense feeling of sadness I had never felt before overcame me. I wished I could live there. Couldn't they just leave me behind? For the first time I'd found some place where I could feel peaceful. Unfortunately, it wasn't mine. That was my reality. I tried to discard my longing for a home like theirs as being ungrateful for what I had.

A few months later I found out that Connor was going to be the lead in his town's high school production that spring. Immediately I wanted to go. Maybe it was his way of wanting to finish what his father had started. I drove an hour and a half to get there. I spoke only a few words to him, congratulating him on what a great job he did, and went straight home to New Jersey afterward.

19

It was February and Suri and I did our best to instill routines in the children's lives despite the unstructured atmosphere. I continued to try and meet the children outside the classroom door each morning so that we could start our interactions the moment we saw each other.

By this point, I finally recognized that I was completely exhausted and this is why I barely had the energy to prepare for the next day. Despite my recognition of this fact, my exhaustion was no excuse to me. I was angry with myself that I could not find a source of energy to draw from. The only reason I felt somewhat justified in experiencing my energy drain was because Suri, who had been there far less time than me, expressed the same feelings. I didn't have a remedy to rejuvenate myself. I didn't go to the teachers lounge for breaks because I didn't have time for breaks. So, I buckled down and did what I had to do, retrieving any energy I could find.

I lived with my college friends at the time, but they didn't want to hear about children so I only spoke of them if something amusing happened at school. A conversation at 22 years old about the worries of parents and their communicatively impaired children was not exactly something of interest to my peers. Besides, at this point I was uncertain of everything and no one wants to spend time complaining because it's just not productive. I felt that I was just getting by at what I was doing, but I wasn't excelling. I didn't want to talk about my insecurities so, like I had done so many times before, I kept my thoughts within.

On top of this emotional exhaustion, I was financially strapped. So, I could do little else but work. On a good day, I would finish work, manage the after school computer program for Judith, and if it was still somewhat light out, go home and go for a run in an attempt to physically run the emotional exhaustion out of me. From there, I would go home and talk to my roommates until I went to bed and then my mind would drift to my class as I fell asleep.

One February morning my class was at work when I looked up to see the occupational therapist at the door. I was always happy to see her because she always had such interesting alternative suggestions for my students' special needs. She had put a few of the children on a strict schedule of "brushing" every morning. The brushing was used to stimulate and calm their bodies. We literally used brushes with soft bristles that, when touched on your skin, felt like someone lightly scratching your back. The brush made it feel softer and more concentrated and allowed you to cover all their tiny limbs in a timely manner. Jonas and Brad were brushed every morning. First thing in the morning, Suri or I would sit next to each child while he played in free time. We would roll up one sleeve at a time, brush an arm and then switch to a leg. The kids rarely resisted because it was calming to them.

Another source of calming for some of the children was wearing a slightly weighted vest. The occupational therapist had taken little cowboy vests and sewn tiny weights into the pockets of each. The slight pressure this put on their bodies increased their bodily control, while soothing them. The vests especially helped during sitting activities. The weight kept them grounded for a greater amount of time than usual. It was similar to the effect of a lead vest that a doctor would put over you before you are X-rayed, but it was much lighter, of course.

We also had large bins of rice and beans, a sandbox, and clay. These were used to promote sensory integration. Brad and Jonas, my two hyperactive children, also wore necklaces like those a teething baby would use. They wore them for different reasons. Jonas constantly bit holes into the bottom of his shirt. He walked or ran around the classroom with his tummy exposed as he pulled the tails of his shirt to his mouth and literally would eat his shirt. Brad, on the other hand, would bite his fists or try to bite other children. The necklaces reduced both of these behaviors a good deal. Instead of biting themselves or things, they bit into the tiny rubber necklace strands that didn't hurt their teeth.

Communicating in pictures helped them whenever it was difficult to translate certain concepts. For instance, one day I brought in shapes from colored poster boards and taped them to the floor. I told the class to line up at the door.

"Andrew, please stand on the red circle. Andrew is standing on the red circle. Jonas, please stand on the blue square. Jonas is standing on the blue square." Then I would state, "We are all in a line. What a beautiful line." By the end of the year they understood what it meant when Miss Maureen told them to "line up."

Some days I would have children climbing up walls and refusing to come down. Sometimes they would just sit on the concrete walkway, almost as if they were collapsing.

I remember one particular day that Michael did this. He decided he did not want to go back into the classroom after recess. He sat down on that concrete. I sat down with him.

"Michael is sitting on the concrete. Michael doesn't want to go back inside. It's OK Michael, let's just sit and rest for a few minutes and then we will go back into the classroom."

I sat with Michael, holding him in my arms the way a mother does her infant child and hugging him on the concrete while the rest of the class was in the school with Suri.

I said, "Michael, it's alright. I know you're scared to come out of yourself, but it's safe here, I promise. You're a good boy. We'll sit here a few more minutes until you're ready to go back inside, OK?" He didn't answer. He didn't need too. I rocked him in my arms until I sensed he was ready.

He was obviously having a hard day; I considered it an accomplishment that he let me hold him in my arms and hug him. We were back in the classroom 30 minutes later.

As we entered the classroom, I thought of how each day really had become less of a challenge. These children were happy to come to school.

Each time I looked at my little ones I could see God in each of them. I believe they sensed this and, as a result, flourished.

I redirected my thoughts and sang, "5 more minutes to work and play, 5 more minutes then we'll put our work away." It took the usual minimum of 10 minutes to get everyone sitting down in a circle. As per the suggestion of the occupational therapist, some would have their weighted vests on, others would have toys in their hands to prevent them from touching other children, and some would sit a few feet away on beanbags.

It was story time as they all sat in the circle. The sequence that we did our tasks in varied each day because the needs and occurrences always varied according to what my children needed that particular day. Therefore, the only routines followed were making sure we "hit" each necessary communication skill. Our day always consisted of sensory integration, general hygiene (like washing hands and brushing teeth after meals), organizational and sequencing skills, hand-eye coordination, and (of course) interactions with each other. I couldn't walk around with a checklist to make sure this happened, nor was I skilled enough to identify whether or not I had covered everything. So, I just smiled and lovingly approached each task, hoping for the best.

20

Mid-semester my freshman year at college, I walked into my apartment to find a message from my dad asking me to call home as soon as possible. I knew instantly something was wrong. First of all, my parents didn't call me at school ever. They didn't want to interfere with my "newfound independence." I had many disagreements with my mom over this philosophy. I was jealous of all my friends whose parents called them at least once a week to see how things were going, how their classes were, if they had enough clothes and money and to just check up in general. My friends received care packages all the time. Their parents seemed interested in their lives. Mine didn't call or send packages. I reasoned that they were too busy but the fact remained: I was on my own.

I picked up the phone knowing that my dad was going to tell me something was wrong.

"Hi, honey. How are you?"

"Fine, what's up?"

"I'm calling with some bad news. Grandpa had a heart attack this morning and he didn't make it."

"Oh my God. I'm sorry, Dad. What happened?"

"He just went to the coat closet in their hallway to get his jacket and he collapsed."

"How is Grandma?"

"She's OK."

"How are you doing?"

"I'm OK, just a lot right now to deal with: the arrangements, the ceremony. The wake is going to be tomorrow and the next day and the funeral the day after. Tucker and Barbara are taking the 11:15

Amtrak train from Union Station up to New Jersey if you want to meet them on it."

"OK, Dad, that is what I'll do."

"OK, love. I'll see you tomorrow, love you."

"Bye. Love you, too."

I cried myself to sleep that night. I was sad for my grandfather but was mostly crying for myself. My grandfather's death was a reason to let myself cry. I cried for my loneliness over the past few months, for my struggle of making new friends, for my inability to figure out how to eat healthily, for my dislike and anxiety I felt sitting in my classes, and for the weight I had gained. I was selfish.

Finally it was acceptable to show unhappiness. I quietly packed my bag. Disgusted with my body I found dress clothes that fit me with the ten extra pounds I had gained. I dreaded seeing my sister and brother on the train and their reaction to my weight gain.

As I got on the train and said hello, Tucker and Barbara gave me a kiss and both looked at me, with what I assumed was dislike as to how I looked with ten extra pounds on me. I felt embarrassed that I was heavy in my eyes and I hated everything around me.

My grandfather's death didn't really hit me until I showed up at the wake. I saw the loss in my grandmother's eyes and her children's. I felt the loss as a grandchild. As I stood in the funeral home talking to my relatives I was finally able to put my own unhappiness aside. I didn't know what I thought about death. I wanted to understand more and feel a sense of peace about what our journey here is about. I was thankful Grandpa had led a long healthy life filled with family and four healthy children.

21

The weeks and months teaching flew by. By late April we were at our full capacity with eight children. Suri was very capable and made things much easier.

The children still wandered and would occasionally leave or, in Jonas' case, sprint out the door despite our best efforts to contain them. As usual, while doing various free play activities, out of the corner of my eye I saw Michael slip out the door. I quickly brought Suri's attention to it but I couldn't go after him until we had regrouped. Michael didn't move anywhere near as fast as Jonas, so I didn't worry about him going too far afield. When I was finally able to leave Suri and the other children, I spotted Michael just as he entered the first grade classroom. By the time I got there the teacher had said hello to Michael and he had walked right past her desk to a calendar. He then read every one of those numbers. Even with my monologue, I could not remove him from the trance-like state he was in. I understood he wasn't trying to be defiant in any way; he just needed to finish, to get to number 31. When he finished, we both turned toward the door. But, just as the words "Michael is finished reading the numbers and we are going back to our classroom" came out of my mouth, he spotted another poster to the right of the door. This had twice the amount of numbers on it and he decided he wanted to add them all up. So, I patiently stood there listening to his math but was unable to communicate with him as I usually did for fear of interrupting the entire classroom that was behind us working. Michael got to the last number and 20 minutes later we were back in our classroom.

I ran into the first grade teacher later that day and apologized for the interruption we had caused earlier. Her own classroom was full of children with learning disabilities, so to some extent we understood one another. To my surprise, however, it was not as much of an understanding as I had thought. She looked at me and said with slight laughter in her voice, "I don't know how you do it."

I smiled back and said, "They're good kids, sometimes difficult, but very good." I have momentary flashbacks of my mother making this statement whenever someone would approach her with the same question.

"I can see that. But, what's the point really? I mean, what's the point with Michael? He is so severe. It's just not worth it."

"Excuse me?"

I was fuming. I couldn't believe what this woman was saying to me; she supposedly taught learning disabled children herself.

Not wanting to get into it, I said, calmly and clearly, "Michael is a very bright boy, he is progressing at a rate that none of his four or more specialists can explain since he's been here." I walked away. I felt I was surrounded once again by people who didn't understand.

I wanted to explain to her but could not compose myself. I wanted to show her the genius in each of my children. I was in defense mode.

She didn't understand that my children seemed to have an overdeveloped sixth sense. They all could sense anger, love, disappointment, disapproval, warmth, trust, and understanding without words. Their biggest challenge was trying to label these feelings. They couldn't explain what each feeling they experienced was, which is where I tried to step in.

It was snack time and the children sat at the circular table. The occupational therapist was in the room observing me handing out snack to each child, making sure everyone had proper chair height, etc. Unlike any other kindergarten classroom, our meals were eaten in silence. I handed out three crackers to each child as usual and, as I continued to the next child, Michael threw his snack down from the table onto the ground. He wanted more crackers and was angry.

Solitary Genius

I walked over and said, "Michael is angry; he is upset. Michael wants more snack, but the rule is we get three crackers." I picked up his food and put it back on the table in front of him. He was upset and just looked at me and continued eating in silence because now he understood.

The OT who was with me had been working with children for over 15 years. I walked back to her to continue to go over some changes and adjustments that would be made. To my surprise she turned to me and said, "My God, that was impressive. You handled that amazingly. I mean, perfectly."

I was surprised to hear that, because I thought I had reacted the way anyone else would have reacted. I simply said, "Thank you." When the children finished their snacks, they knew to throw away their garbage and wash their hands. The children loved to go to the water fountain that was a few feet outside of our classroom. So, this was another opportunity for communication. They would start out with just the request, "Water fountain," and then we would expand with, "Water fountain, please," and build up to, "Can I go to the water fountain, please?" The interesting thing was that when I would tell some of my children's parents what our exercises were they would suggest that these tasks were too simple for their children. I felt sorry for the parents' misperceptions of what their children needed versus the reality I experienced. As I helped one child wash up Emma scampered up to me and said, "Water fountain please," with her pretty blue eyes and a lovely smile.

"Thank you for asking so nicely Emma. You may go to the water fountain."

I looked away, helping out the other children, and when I looked up I discovered I was down one more child, Michael.

He certainly hadn't asked me to go anywhere, so I said to my Godsend of an aide, "I'll be right back."

As I rushed out my classroom door I looked over at the water fountain to find our extra-tall Michael pressing the water fountain button for our extra-tiny Emma. Now, seeing is believing, and no one can or will tell me that these children cannot see outside of themselves. They can. You just have to believe in them, just as I needed someone to believe in me all those years of grade school.

Despite the energy that these wonderful triumphs gave us, Suri and I were both scrambling to do the work of what at least three people should have been doing. As a result, we were utterly exhausted by the spring. We began to count the days because it was just too much for us to handle. I was maxed out and the only people who really understood were Suri and one other speech pathology assistant, Rachel, who I had become friends with. She saw increments of what really went on each day and if she had a break in her day she was kind enough to pop in and help. My energy was really totally depleted.

I just felt like I couldn't do it one more day, but had told myself I had to be there for the children. I wanted a day to myself, for myself. I was in overdrive in order to keep going. None of my children had ever seen or heard me raise my voice but I snapped that one day. Michael was sitting closest to me and he had one of his books in hand. I had prompted him twice that we were closing the book and going outside for snack. I wanted him to do what I wanted at that moment and raised my voice the third time with impatience and aggression, "Finished!" He did not react. Instead, he looked at me, let me close the book and just stared into my eyes lovingly as he got up from the floor. I wanted to cry; I knew then that he trusted me and felt safe in my care. He had just done for me what I did for him everyday.

22

If I needed a break outside of work I did what I could afford. I visited my mother's house. While I was teaching I was in my family's life on a regular basis. With Judith's input, I had become so in tune with classifying and categorizing observations of disorder and dysfunction that each time I went home I couldn't help but analyze what was going on in the house that I had grown up in. I would take my new understanding with me to New Jersey and would come back asking Judith questions. This was when I made the connection that much as my students' families unintentionally contributed to their disorders, my family was also a factor in my struggles, and I slowly distanced myself more than I ever had before.

I identified one of those factors one winter day when I went to visit. I walked into the house that afternoon to find the tropical temperature I expected. To me it was as warm as I could imagine the womb of a mother is to her fetus.

"Is anyone warm in here?" I stripped down as much as I could and then I'd ask around.

Half say they are suffocating and half say they are comfortable. I crack a window or door and stick as closely to it as I can. This unhealthy warmth signified to me the unhealthy suffocation I had felt as a child.

I try to shrug it off. I try not to become tired and want to sleep like so many of my siblings do at random hours during the day. I never knew it <u>wasn't</u> normal for children to sleep all day long. Happy children don't want to sleep, they have an internal drive in them and want to play and do things with friends. I had always been given the explanation by my mother that these are growing girls or boys and that is why they are sleeping so much. I thought that made sense and I accepted it. Now I no longer accept that explanation.

Now, when a home I walk into has a drastic climate to it - either very warm or very cold - this is my first clue that something in general is off balance. I walk up to my mother's room to say hello. She gives me a clingy hug. Just like the suffocating house. I imagine she wants to suffocate me with kisses like the mother of an infant who can't control herself from kissing every ounce of her newborn.

"I'm so happy you are home." I smile and don't say a word. I have mixed feelings. I am happy to visit the home I grew up in, but at the same time I am unsure as to whether or not I like the energy of this home. I keep these hurtful thoughts to myself. I am careful with my words. It is important to me to say the truth and not lie just to please my mother or anyone for that matter. Probably a trait I have learned from my parents. I do not ever want to feel regret that I was not true to my word. I can't say cliché things like, "You are the best," or, "I couldn't have done it without you," unless, in my heart, I truly believe these things to be true. My mother cuts into my thoughts again.

"I have to run to the grocery store. Is there anything that you want?"

"No, that's kind of you to ask. Thanks, Mom. I meant to ask you, is Anthony liking school anymore than he was?"

Anthony, the youngest, was in first grade at the time.

"No, not really."

"Mom, he just has a little bit of a learning disability, like I did. He has a processing and word retrieval problem. I can see it. Just enroll him in the computer program that we run and he'll do better."

She responded, "He's smart though, he'll be fine."

"Mom, I know he'll be fine, but why should he just be fine when if he is given a little nudge he can be happy?"

"Let's just give him some more time."

Despite the fact that I was speaking to my own mother, she resisted my advice, like any parent would. No one wants to admit the reality of their child's challenges.

Mom lowers her voice to a whisper, "You know Mo, I just wanted to mention something else."

"What's that?"

"It's Tim. He walked in here about two weeks ago and laid down on our bed right before school and said, 'I think I'm depressed.' Of course, your father and I said, 'Well, we will deal with this like any illness. Let's take you to the doctor.'"

I am amazed that she is saying this but on the other hand, what other way do you deal with a child <u>telling</u> you that he needs help?

"So, we took him to a very good psychiatrist and, of course, your father and I couldn't be in the room, but the doctor told us that he is very down. I mean, VERY down. Do you think you might be able to talk to him a bit? You always seem to be able to talk to your siblings. He's just not a big talker and I think if you...."

"Sure, Mom. Just a couple of things: has he gone back to the shrink or is he going back soon?"

"He went that one time and said he won't go back again."

"Why not?"

"He just refuses."

"I'll talk to him."

"Thank you, honey."

"Where is he now?"

"I think he's sleeping."

I sit at the kitchen table sipping some tea when Tim walks in. He had just woken up from his unnecessary daytime nap.

"Hi Tim."

"Hey."

He bends over to review the dozen boxes of cereal that are in my mother's cabinets.

"How are you?"

"Fine."

"How's school?"

"Fine."

From his posture, his monotone voice, and his responses I conclude how miserable he is.

"You don't seem fine, Tim. You seem unhappy."

He has no response as he sits opposite me at the kitchen table.

"You know, Timmy, school is not easy. I hated grade school and high school wasn't that much better. I coped with high school a little bit better but it definitely wasn't the happiest time."

He just looks up at me as he shovels spoonfuls of Captain Crunch into his mouth. He is not rejecting what I am saying so I slowly continue my conversation, pausing just like one pauses to digest when eating. He, however, is not pausing at all from his bowl. He is just shoveling it into his mouth without a breath.

"Just so you know, when I was in school, I always looked at people as if they were acting immature and I was annoyed. It wasn't easy but I got through it and when you get to college it gets a little bit better. Most of all, I guess I felt like I was alone, like no one really thought the way I did, and that is a hard way to live but it gets better. It really does."

He gets up, puts his bowl in the sink and glances at me quickly, much like my students, unable to respond.

Weeks later my mother asked me what I had said to Timothy that day. I told her I just spoke to him about when I was in school.

She responded with tears in her eyes, "Well, whatever you said, I think you saved his life."

Each time I had seen Tim prior to that conversation, I actually hadn't seen him because he was always "napping." Whenever he wasn't napping he would complain to me about school and how tired he was from his commute. As each year of high school went by, Timmy slept more and more. I identified it as the inability to deal with life, much as it had been for me as a child. The root of his sleeping habit was sadness; he was shutting everything out. I could also see that my mother and father felt helpless as to what should be done. I could only see the many parallels between the internalizations my brother was experiencing and those of my students.

23

What one would call subtle changes in behavior resulted in major changes within the classroom. They were so subtle to the outside world that I often would have to remind myself of them. These children were unique in so many ways but when it comes down to it, we are all the same, and I found and focused on those similarities.

Each and every one of those children had gone through a time when I had to repeat a direction multiple times as I guided them to do it. When I was feeling exhausted at the end of the year, I had to say to myself, look, I may have had to be repetitive, but look at the outcome.

Another subtle sign of their progress in becoming connected was the fact that there was a time that they played alone with no acknowledgment of the outside world. Children would now walk up to other children as they completed a task. Some children were now verbalizing their desire to be included in a task and some just put their bodies there because that, in itself, was a huge gesture of connection. But, actions do speak louder than words and it would only be a matter of time for those actions to form into words. Children who would hide in a particular task that was their favorite no longer did so to such an extreme. For example, Michael loved his books and his way of retreating when he couldn't handle things was to sit with his book in a chair and read. He would drown himself in that book to shut the world out. He no longer immersed himself in those books he had read so many times that he had them all memorized. Instead, he would sit with the book on his lap and just observe his peers. This was a huge step for him. It showed that he was interested in his peers and the outside world. He was looking outside of himself and if he needed a break every once in a while with a book which served as his security blanket, then that was perfectly acceptable.

The daily behaviors of these children were like that of any other, filled with emotions and feelings, hard days and easy days. We had become accustomed to behaviors such as children lying on the floor, sometimes rolling on the floor. Others might dance randomly throughout the day. Sometimes a child would yell out randomly. A lot of it was short periods of compulsive behavior in some form. Whether it be picking at something on their skin or outfit or using a toy over and over again. To me, this signified the need to explore their behavior. I would be sure to verbalize what they were doing while they were doing it. Eventually, the words would sink in, and at that point something would shift in their behavior.

When it came to being outdoors, many children would wander off, content to be on their own, away from their peers. Throughout the year, the distance between them would gradually decrease and before long, they became a group. Then, they progressed to acknowledging one another's presence by looking at them or tapping them in some way. Sometimes, they would just smile and stay close; these were all major accomplishments.

Transitioning from one task to another was always a challenge, especially if we had to leave the classroom. In the beginning, there was always a child who didn't get up to follow the group, but this resistance was no longer an issue by the end of the year because these kids no longer wanted to be separated from their peers. They had become a family, one that wanted to be close. These children used what they were most gifted with, their senses. They felt accepted and, therefore, sensed love in that classroom.

Of course, the most obvious signs of improvement were when my children would walk up to me or a peer and verbalize without my having to prompt them for words. Other signs of major progress were when they would actually state their feelings clearly or, even more miraculously, sit with one another and laugh, sharing moments of humor.

I remember one particular day when Jonas was playing and his Kippah fell off his head and onto the floor. Michael noticed this and very clandestinely picked it up and put it on his own head. A few minutes later I heard Jonas asking, "Where's my Kippah? Where's my Kippah?" I knew Michael was acting as if he didn't hear his question. Both Suri and I could see what Jonas couldn't because he was significantly shorter than Michael. We laughed at the situation. Of course, we had to step in.

"Michael, you need to give Jonas his Kippah back."

Before he could respond in any way Jonas had quickly jumped up and grabbed it off Michael's head. It was refreshing to have such "normal" predicaments to deal with.

By the end of the year, every one of my children, when called upon by name, would turn their heads immediately and look at me. I would be amazed when a visitor would come into my classroom and a child would look up and say hello. This made it so clear to me how much they were accepting the outside world. They were becoming happy children.

Almost every one of the children struggled a great deal with their hand-eye coordination. In order to decrease any difficulties they might have, we made sure we had the extra fat crayons or markers and, as a result, avoided a great deal of frustration for them.

My children liked to hum and sing. One day I decided I would sing along and use it as a lesson. I began to sing the words with my students and as they walked away from me I continued singing with them. When the children finished the song and turned around and looked at me with a smile I knew my lesson was successful. They acknowledged that they were paying attention to me joining in and that I was happily a part of their world.

Computer time was implemented later in the year when they were more capable of working as a group. As with any child, taking and waiting for their turn was difficult. I was careful to limit this time because I knew that TV and computers were a major outlet for these children to just sit and not interact, going against exactly what we were trying to accomplish. The reality of the situation was that TV and computers were a part of their daily lives and, therefore, I had some of my most extreme behavioral reactions from my children during this time. The children got so sucked in that they had a greater difficulty stopping themselves from playing and allowing the next child to take the mouse. Some children would cry because their time had ended. Others would laugh hysterically because of something they viewed on the screen. I think a major reason these children became so emotionally involved in those games was that they didn't fully grasp the reality vs. non-reality of what we were dealing with.

24

The school year had just ended and I was wrapping up some final things as I reflected on my year. I wanted to climb out of my life just like Michael climbed that tree one day. We had just had lunch and we were outside for recess. There was a brick wall about four feet high surrounding the playground. We were constantly getting children down from the wall. They loved to walk along it, giving them a clear view from the perimeter of the entire playground.

It was busy outside because nearly the entire school was out enjoying the beautiful day. There was a large group of children playing baseball and many of my students were watching the "older kids" from the sidelines. I looked around, counting up my little ones, and I noticed that we were missing Michael.

I went to Suri, "Have you seen Michael?"

She hadn't. The next minute, I found myself looking up a large old tree that overlooked the playground. He had climbed up the wall and grabbed onto the tree, continuing to climb. In my head, I said, oh shit. I didn't feel like climbing trees today. Working with these kids, my wardrobe was significantly limited. I had to wear slacks every day because I never knew what predicament I would end up in and I had to make sure I had shoes on that I could run and climb in.

I started my usual monologue, "Michael is in the tree. Michael needs to come down now."

He climbed one branch higher. I said, sternly, "Michael, you need to come down."

Next thing I knew, I started climbing the tree and was feeling a bit overwhelmed with the height and whether or not I would be able to get myself down, let alone Michael. Needless to say, I'd already begun praying.

Apparently it worked because reinforcement was sent, and next thing I knew, the fit, young and handsome gym teacher had noticed my predicament and as quickly as he graciously offered his help I was out of that tree. John ended up climbing up, talking to Michael, and getting him down.

I wished I could stand on that wall right then and just review the year, like a movie. I still had so many doubts about my abilities that I found myself reverting to some very old behaviors.

I drove home one July day after tutoring all day and I lay down on my bed, feeling like I could collapse. I was depressed and felt trapped. The exhaustion I had kept at bay all year came bearing down on me and I knew, with intense certainty, that my work at the school was done. My gut told me to call my cousin, Phyllis. Within a month I was in New York City with a new world in front of me.

The phone calls that I would place to or receive from Judith over the following years were incredibly affirming. I remember one day she called and said, "Maureen, the new teacher is now using the positive reinforcement reward system that the rest of the school uses but it's not working and she keeps asking me what you did in that classroom. They just don't understand. They can't do what you did." It was the compliment and recognition she had never really expressed while I was working for her. I felt relief. I had done something right.

About two years went by until I spoke with Judith again. We had a long and involved conversation on the phone that day that shocked me.

"Judith, I don't even know what that means. What are they doing to this poor child?"

"It's a medical procedure. They basically take all the blood out and remove all the 'toxins,' like mercury. Then they put the blood back into his body. It's very controversial."

I clench my jaw, horrified by what Judith has just said.

"Why are they doing this?"

She responds in the matter-of-fact, professional voice I know so well, "They're desperate and don't know what else to do."

"I can't believe people are treating autistic children like we treated mental patients in the '70s. That's horrible."

"I know, Maureen."

"Why can't people understand that it's not about the mercury in their blood or their diet?"

"Maureen, people can't always see what we see."

"Come on Judith, you know every professional on the East Coast, every neurologist, child psychologist and speech pathologist. Who among these professionals you know 'get' autistic children like we do?"

I am expecting her to tell me a handful of professionals and maybe convince them to volunteer for the cause.

"Honestly? No one."

The words start to sink in. Why is she telling this to me now? Why didn't she say this 5 years ago when I was working with her?

"Maureen, you are the only person I know who can see what I see. It's not something you can learn; it's just something you have. I have my Ph.D. in speech pathology with a specialty in neurological communication disorders, but those degrees are not what allow me to really understand these children. I know you have struggled in the past 5 years with trying to figure out what to do with your life but this is your calling. You created miracles when you were working here in Baltimore. Real-life miracles. Michael was your biggest miracle. So few people know or understand what you really did. The parents don't even really know and won't ever know. But, I know."

I feel relieved and respond with a heartfelt, "Thanks, Judith." Despite my feelings, maybe I truly am talented.

"Anyway Judith, you won't believe this but I'm sitting in a hospital parking lot in Long Island going to visit my cousin right now and it is almost 8:15 P.M. I really love talking with you about this but will miss visiting hours if I don't get off soon."

"Of course, I'll call you next time I'm in Manhattan and we'll try and meet up for lunch."

"That would be great, good night."

"Good night Maureen. You are such a good girl."

"Thanks, Judith."

I want to cry because this conversation reminded me how well we did and can connect. Most importantly, I am reminded of the fact that this connection created miracles that neither of us could have created on our own.

The conversation lingers as I visit my cousin, drive home to my New York City apartment and finally fall asleep. Judith telling me that no one else understands these children haunts my every thought. Had I made a wrong turn in my life? Why did I leave those kids who understood me and vice versa? I left because in my gut I felt the need to move on. I felt as poorly understood as the autistic children I was teaching. It has taken years to understand what made these successes possible. There are multiple answers that boil down to one. Through alternative ways of searching for an understanding I have found I have major sensitivities to my environment. I have also been told by professionals that I am extremely intuitive myself and as a result function on a different frequency which is the main cause of these sensitivities and at the same time, allowed me to communicate with these children who are also on a different frequency. I can't prove any of this. The only thing I can prove is that these children progressed substantially.

I do know that I often feel like my kids must have felt when they would just put their entire bodies in the huge bin of dried beans and corn. They needed the tactile. It was a normal thing to walk into my classroom and find a child sitting in an entire bin of dried corn, another child in sand, and another in dried rice and beans. Most people would say to a child, no, the bin is to put your hands in. In theory that is what the intention of it was but the first day I saw one of my children just sit down smack in the middle of it, I chuckled to myself and left him there. That stimuli that surrounded their bodies centered and calmed them from the stimuli outside themselves. That is what I feel that I need these days. I constantly say I need to go to the spa (so do most of my friends for that matter). Maybe it's not the spa we really need but a bin full of dried beans and rice to calm and ground us.

The point is that I had to learn to feel and experience things on my own in my own way just like my autistic children did. Autism and the other disorders I was exposed to that year all fall under the category of an extreme communication disorder. Isn't society in general just as prone to these extreme behaviors? We have extreme diets, extreme cases of depression, extreme drugs, extreme shows dominate our televisions, extreme adventures and sports, extreme technology. We are constantly being bombarded by stimulants. We can't turn on our email without five ads popping up. We can't watch TV without having another program on in the corner of the screen. Our computers have 5 different things minimized so that we can access them at a moment's notice. We are increasingly unfocused, floating more and more through life unaware, missing things. These children are floating as well. It seems we are becoming numb, almost like we're being culturally driven into autism. Perhaps they are an extreme version of ourselves in 20 years if we don't change something.

Silence seems nonexistent unless we choose it. Most of all, I have learned from all of this that the greatest source of healing for others, my children and even myself has been <u>being listened to.</u> Listening in every sense of the word. Listening to one's inner reality, listening to one's senses, to how things make one feel, to what makes one feel good and inspires them. My communicatively impaired children slowed me down enough so that I could learn this truth.

Children seem to understand more than adults do about life. I know as a child I instinctively understood the value of silence. But, at the same time, I was angry because of the seclusion and frustration of my state. What if this is just how an autistic child, a learning disabled child or a depressed child views things? What if they have cut themselves off from the world because they are angry, trapped, and fearful? If so, what if we look at an autistic child as a hurt being (even when they have uncontrollable actions such as tantrums)? Would there be greater results from this approach and could we slowly transform them to desire life outside of the shield they have created by doing so?

I have my own hypothesis about my own life and why I connected so profoundly with these children. First I had to figure out how my brain worked and who I was. I also had to learn to take care of myself. Then I could learn how to communicate. This is what I believe autistic children need to do as well. They need to learn who they are. Don't focus on the outcome, which in most eyes would be speech. Focus on the <u>process</u>. The process would be the experience of feeling. Just like an infant has to feel things and touch them and explore them before he or she speaks. For some reason, children with severe communication disorders have shut themselves down mid-process and thus, communication halts. Something has created darkness for these children.

I could not guarantee success of the program nor could the school or Judith. I can only tell my honest experience and how I approached what so much of society categorizes as profound. I looked at each child as normal, soul to soul, spirit to spirit. They were not impaired in my eyes, <u>never.</u> So many people have opinions and facts about autism and severe communication disorders, but the only real truth lies within the child, only he has the answer. And in my eyes, that secret can only be unlocked by compassionate and patient nurturing.

Finally, the answer became clear: the entire year I had unconsciously done exactly what Judith needed me to do through effort and understanding, creating an art form. Art heals, and the children's progress was proof of this. Judith explained the "innate art form" to me as clinically as she could: I had worked at the child's pace, I had built trust, I added on to the child's actions and words, I knew when to back off, and I built sequencing skills all through natural play. This is what had caused Judith to give me the independence she did. In fact, she had applied those same principles with me. I just couldn't "see" it.

25

Andrew eventually "normalized" and was mainstreamed into a "regular" classroom the following year. About a year later, I saw Michael and, with effort, he was speaking complete sentences. I don't know where the others went or where they are now. My brother Sean is a surgeon. Lizzie, who had the disheveled side of our bedroom as kids, is also a surgeon. Her brain saw order in what I could not and her choice of profession is evidence of this. Tim got through his schooling and writes. Anthony ended up taking the computerized program and is an honors student. Cousin Phyllis, who, unbeknownst to her, I prayed for as a child, became a mentor and like a mother to me. She has passed on to the other side, and left with me the answer to the greater part of living. And finally, that confused internalized child seems just like that, a child from long ago.

Finally, I have lived in NYC for over ten years now, and it is one of the most chaotic and stimulating places on earth. I have worked in some of the most demanding jobs in this city. Entertainment, creative jobs and even working at a hedge fund have been my focus over the years. I'm sure the many people I have worked with could almost not imagine the Mo who is spoken of in these pages because I multi-task all day long, and have a level of energy that is hard to match. Most importantly, I love my life. I love the pace and energy of this city and, more than anything, I love to see the pictures that unfold in front of me each and every day.

Acknowledgements

I have so many people to thank for this book. I have done my best to list them below, but we all know there is always that one person who we forget and want to kick ourselves in the butt for forgetting. So, I will thank that person first. I have to thank my editors next because without them, what was a bunch of pages would not have become a book. So thank you to…

My Editors:

Rachel Safko - The first official edit - a mound of papers that you passionately dedicated time and effort to as if it was your own; I will never forget you for that.

Linda Kahn - An amazing editor. I thank you for your belief in my talent and assurance that this would be the first of many.

Hillary Wohl – for your dedication to me and your professional knowledge.

Mike Marshall - for your genuine concern, love and edits!

Emily Heckman - for the endurance you brought back to me in getting the final details done and countless words of wisdom in making it all come together.

My Family:

Mom and Dad - the title "mom and dad" alone is enough, thank you.

Matt Marshall - the amazing reference point that you always are.

Sean Marshall - for setting up my website and making it real.

The rest of the Marshalls - Bill, Samantha, Connor, Brendan, Kieran, Cate, Misty, Michael Jr.,Copeland, Elizabeth, Annie, Laura, Sean & Christopher – for inspiring me.

Phyllis Huffman DelVecchio- Critic who was a mom to me. The first person I let take a look at a shapeless manuscript and who said to "keep at it."

Jules DelVecchio - The classiest person I know who treats every individual as the special person they are. You inspire me, care so genuinely, and are another dad to me.

Friends who are like family:
Michelle Bicocchi Thyen - for your endless support and enthusiasm.

Julia Trintis, Jill Moeller, Anna Faunlagui, Megan Kaplan, Ellen Costa Butera, Mandie DeVincentis, Alanna Campbell, Alaine Aldaffer, James Calleri, Crystal Jenkins, Cuky Harvey, Lise Fisher, Dorothy Aaronson, Richard Medley, Meredith Field, Terry Weaver, Jaime Schlesinger, Dan DiPierro, Mindi Yuspeh, TYou Canoe, AND everyone else's path that I have been blessed to pass and got me where I am today.

Design Team:
Catherine Haggarty – Artwork – you are so talented.

Sean Sutherland - Cover design – another talented one!

www.solitarygenius.com

Solitary Genius can be purchased at:

www.iUniverse.com

www.bn.com

www.amazon.com